THE TECHNOLOGY TOOLBELT FOR TEACHING

Susan Manning and Kevin E. Johnson

JOSSEY-BASS
A Wiley Imprint
www.josseybass.com

Published by Jossey-Bass
A Wiley Imprint
989 Market Street, San Francisco, CA 94103-1741—www.josseybass.com

Jossey-Bass books and products are available through most bookstores. To contact Jossey-Bass directly call our Customer Care Department within the U.S. at 800-956-7739, outside the U.S. at 317-572-3986, or fax 317-572-4002.

Jossey-Bass also publishes its books in a variety of electronic formats. Some content that appears in print may not be available in electronic books.

Library of Congress Cataloging-in-Publication Data

Manning, Susan, 1960-
    The technology toolbelt for teaching / Susan Manning, Kevin E. Johnson. — 1st ed.
        p. cm. — (The Jossey-Bass Higher and adult education series)
    Includes bibliographical references and index.
    ISBN 978-0-470-63424-0 (pbk.)
    ISBN 978-1-118-00518-7 (ebk.)
    ISBN 978-1-118-00519-4 (ebk.)
    ISBN 978-1-118-00520-0 (ebk.)
    1. Educational technology. 2. Computer-assisted instruction. I. Johnson, Kevin E. II. Title.
    LB1028.3.M36 2011
    371.33′4—dc22

                                                                    2010046962

Printed in the United States of America
FIRST EDITION
PB Printing   10 9 8 7 6 5 4 3 2 1

CONTENTS

THE JOSSEY-BASS HIGHER AND ADULT

EDUCATION SERIES

Teaching is not easy, and teaching with technology is a little like trying to hit a moving target. Tools change, versions are updated, and few of us have time to completely analyze and thoughtfully render what that means for instruction. This book is dedicated to the brave teachers who do their best at integrating technology.

And as we did in our first book, we would like to dedicate this book to our families. We didn't get this far without good guidance from our parents, and we couldn't have worked through the development of this book without awesome support from our husbands and children.

PREFACE

Susan has a neighbor who has every tool imaginable in his garage. When residents on the street start home improvement projects, they first visit Fred's garage and have a conversation with him about what they need and what they might borrow from him. He doesn't try to convince them to buy a table saw when what they really need to borrow is a hacksaw to trim a 1-inch piece of PVC pipe. Fred understands that tools should be used in a specific context for a specific purpose. He saves the neighbors time, aggravation, and money.

That is exactly what this book is about, except that the context is technology tools. Instead of coming into Fred's garage, you will come to us with instructional problems that *might* be solved with technology.

Today's instructors feel pressured to integrate technology into their traditional or online instruction, but they're not quite sure what to do or why they should use these tools. With the proliferation of free or inexpensive Web-based tools, the pressure to be "cool and tech savvy" seems even greater. Teachers who incorporate new tools into their instruction are perceived to be cutting-edge. Those who do not embrace tools are sometimes viewed as unfavorably resistant. Rather than taking sides, this book examines how teachers might use technology tools to address instructional problems.

The caveat is that whatever tools teachers choose to incorporate must be part of the instructional design from the beginning, not cool add-ons. If tools do not address specific instruction problems, they are worthless. What sets our book apart from others is that we provide a decision-making process, a matrix, with which teachers can examine individual tools and determine whether these tools can truly address the instructional needs. We only introduce tools as a means to carry out pedagogy.

Our Audience

We wrote this book for the broadest market of instructors: those who teach in higher education and those who teach in elementary and secondary schools. That may appear to be too wide a scope. However, we believe that whether you work with our youngest or oldest learners, the twenty-first century demands some inclusion of technology. Very quickly those twelve-year-olds in middle school who know how to surf the Internet and view what they want on YouTube are going to be coming into higher education classrooms looking for some inclusion of media.

We wrote this book for both online instructors and those who teach in traditional classrooms. It may be easier to see the application of some tools for a wholly online course, but many of these tools are still appropriate for a brick-and-mortar setting. They may be tools that are used by the teacher in the classroom or tools that are used by the students at home.

Organization

This book is organized by themes. In Part One we lay the foundation for using tools in the context of instructional design. We begin in Chapter One with an overview of instructional technology and the Internet, considering such popular themes as Web 2.0 and where are headed in the future. In Chapter Two we introduce several models of instructional design and tie these to the selection process for technology tools. In doing so, we offer a Decision-Making Matrix and a supplemental guide of questions that teachers can use to examine technology tools and deliberately consider whether these tools support their pedagogy. The Decision-Making Matrix is used throughout the book.

Part Two introduces an array of tools that address problems of organization. Teachers who are disorganized lose valuable time and resources. Chapter Three introduces calendaring tools that can help manage time. Chapter Four contributes to time management with scheduling tools that allow multiple parties to arrange meetings. Chapter Five introduces readers to mind maps or graphic organizers, Web-based tools that help organize thoughts and ideas. Staying organized with bookmarks and favorite Web sites is the dominion of social bookmarking, the topic for Chapter Six. Chapter Seven addresses tools that can help manage digital or virtual documents or files, some of which may be quite large and unwieldy. (For example, where do you put a 100 MB movie?)

Part Three continues our discussion of Web-based tools by introducing the idea of using these tools to communicate and collaborate. Such tools can encourage instructor-to-instructor, instructor-to-student, student-to-student, and guest-to-class communication and collaboration efforts. We begin with what may be the most popular tool in online education—discussion forums. Chapter Eight looks at both text-based and voice-enabled discussion tools. Chapter Nine specifically addresses Voice over Internet Protocol (VoIP) tools, which allow parties to talk to each other in a manner similar to using a telephone. Imagine having your class talk to a class halfway across the globe! Instant messaging and chat programs are the focus of Chapter Ten. Not only do these tools make faculty more accessible to students but also students can use them to complete academic work. Chapter Eleven examines blogs and their instructional uses, whereas Chapter Twelve considers wikis for collaborative work. Microblogs as instructional tools are discussed in Chapter Thirteen. Chapter Fourteen introduces Web conferencing, allowing real-time communication between students and teachers with visual and audio components.

Part Four addresses an ongoing dilemma for online instructors—finding ways to present content when teaching online. This is one area in which students bring relatively high expectations given the sophisticated media they see online in other contexts. In Chapter Fifteen we address audio tools, such as podcasts. Chapter Sixteen adds video to the instructional mix. Screencasting, one specialized form of video presentation, is introduced in Chapter Seventeen. Chapter Eighteen looks at the ever-popular narrated slideshow. Chapter Nineteen, which considers graphics and images, reinforces the idea that a picture is worth a thousand words.

The age-old question of how teachers assess learning is the focus of Part Five. Traditional tools for assessment, including quizzes, surveys, and online tests, are examined in Chapter Twenty. Chapter Twenty-One looks at rubrics and matrixes that may be used to evaluate performance-based or authentic assessment. The topic of e-portfolios rounds out our discussion of assessment tools in Chapter Twenty-Two.

Part Six concludes our tour of tools with those that help transform identity, tools that are uniquely twenty-first century. These are technologies that were not available to the average teacher or student ten years ago. Chapter Twenty-Three examines the use of avatars. Chapter Twenty-Four considers virtual worlds. Finally, Chapter Twenty-Five looks at social networking and the online identities of students and teachers.

What This Book Is Not

This book is not a comprehensive listing of every tool available. It is not a sales guide for one product over another. Because technology changes so quickly and products move from beta to market (or disappear) within a matter of months, we have limited the number of tools. For each category, we have tried to select several tools that we think have some longevity and that will meet teachers' needs. Most important, we apply our Decision-Making Matrix to a couple of specific tools per chapter to model how instructors might consider additional tools they find in their own research.

How to Read This Book

Hearkening back to the example of Susan's neighbor, we suggest that you read this book with an instructional problem in mind. In other words, if you're going to visit our garage and ask about a tool, consider a project you want to tackle so you can ask for the right tool. First read Chapters One and Two so that you understand the framework of the following chapters and how to use the Decision-Making Matrix. From there, jump to whatever chapter you believe is best going to solve your instructional problem. You do not need to read this book in a linear fashion! It may be interesting, however, to stay within certain parts so that you can see how tools are designed to address one problem better than others.

ACKNOWLEDGMENTS

We would like to acknowledge the friends who have helped us experiment with the tools and lent their faces for screenshots. We also came into contact with several innovative companies, such as TweenTribune and Edmodo. In the technology world, it's rewarding to find a tool and meet the people behind the technology.

We would also like to thank Erin Null, Alison Knowles, and the editing team for making us look so good.

ABOUT THE AUTHORS

Susan Manning is best known as a teacher's teacher. She develops faculty and prepares them to teach online. Susan teaches online courses for the University of Wisconsin at Stout and the University of Illinois' Illinois Online Network in online learning, instructional design, technology tools, the synchronous classroom, and group work online. She has taught hundreds of teachers, including international instructors from Saudi Arabia, Denmark, Vietnam, and Russia. Susan's teaching career began with adult students learning English as a second language, and she often introduced them to new technologies she thought could help them learn. These students reminded her that basic human interaction and communication skills always trump technology.

Susan's online career began more than ten years ago when she became an online student and earned her certification as Master Online Teacher from the University of Illinois. In addition, she holds a doctorate in adult education from Ball State University, a master's in college student personnel from Bowling Green State University, and a bachelor's degree in communications from Truman State University.

Susan also puts her teaching and development skills to work as a producer for LearningTimes, LLC. Susan helps coordinate synchronous online conferences, but her favorite role is training presenters to enter the brave new world of presenting online. Finally, she can be heard regularly on the LearningTimes Green Room podcast, a series she cohosts with friend Dan Balzer as they examine issues and topics related to learning.

Kevin E. Johnson is CEO of the Cutting Ed, Inc., a consulting company that specializes in helping clients envision education and training for the twenty-first century. He has more than twenty years of experience working in education and figuring out how to use technology to his advantage.

Kevin started with technology as a fourteen-year-old teaching himself to program. Completing his bachelor's degree at Eastern Illinois University and his master's at the University of Illinois, Kevin developed curriculum and taught in academic and corporate environments for the next thirteen years. Due to his desire to save paper (not to mention not wanting to fight for the copy machine), he started providing lecture notes and other resources to students on CDs. As the Internet emerged, he began teaching Web development courses. It was a natural transition to move from burning CDs to placing course content on the Web. Before long, Kevin was interacting with his students electronically, and his interest in online education began.

PART ONE

INTRODUCTION

In our opening chapters we lay the foundation for using tools in the context of instructional design. We begin in Chapter One with an overview of instructional technology and sort through the definitions of technology and educational technology. We then review the development of the Internet as most of us recall it, considering such popular concepts as Web 2.0. What distinguished Web 2.0 from Web 1.0 largely had to do with the ability to interact with and change content, to share and subscribe (for example, to Really Simple Syndication [RSS] feeds), and the granular nature of content. For example, an English instructor could share a learning object on correct APA citation styles, which could be dropped into a variety of science courses to address that one point. What we do in the future will depend on how the Web continues to develop.

In Chapter Two we introduce several models of instructional design and tie these to the selection process for technology tools. Herein we assert that *technology tools must be used in the context of instructional design*. We therefore offer a Decision-Making Matrix and resource that suggests more questions teachers should ask as they examine technology tools and deliberately consider whether these tools support their pedagogy. We explain the nuances of these questions and their implications as you move forward in the book.

CHAPTER ONE

WHY WEB-BASED TOOLS?

For generations, wise old sages have enjoyed telling youngsters about life before the latest innovation, invention, or technology. Teachers are no different. First we told stories about life before the printing press when knowledge was only transmitted orally, then about how students had to write their own notes because we did not have copy machines to reproduce the latest handout, and now we pass on stories about life before the Internet when no one could "Google." And with every invention of new technology and tools, in true teacher fashion, we scratch our heads and wonder where this is leading. In what ways do the latest innovations enhance learning and assist teachers in doing so?

That is the fundamental purpose of this book. We are going to explore a variety of technology tools available to teachers with an eye to instructional design and delivery. It is not enough to know that gizmos and gadgets exist—we must also consider how tools might be used to address instructional problems.

Defining Technology

Before we get too far into the text, we should first define technology, instructional or educational technology, and technology tools. We will address these definitions again in Chapter Two when we relate these to instructional design.

Science and technology are sometimes mentioned in the same breath, but there are notable differences. Science often deals with outcomes that are directly observable through the senses (Arms & Camp, 1998); teaching and learning do not. A better way to look at technology is to consider the International Network for Small and Medium Enterprises' definition of technology as "human innovation in action that involves the generation of knowledge and processes to develop systems that solve problems and extend human capabilities" (2010, p. 1). There may be a science behind how the technology works (such as computer science), and the application to solve problems may be systematic, but the results are not always so neatly observable as to be classified according to our senses.

Employing instructional or educational technology, therefore, is the process by which we use tools to address an instructional problem. This is not new science. As Saettler (2004) reminds us, instructional technology dates far back. Today's examples of technology include communication through e-mail and Voice over Internet Protocol, streaming video and content presentations, and synchronous Web conferencing, to name a few. All of these technologies can support learning as they address instructional problems. Further, if technology is a process, then the specific tools are the instruments we use to implement that process. Skype, YouTube, and Elluminate are specific tools that demonstrate the implementation of the previous examples.

The technology we examine in this book falls into the realm of educational technology in that we will discuss processes by which specific tools are applied to instructional problems. This is increasingly relevant in higher education as more and more courses become "distributed," either as fully online courses or blended courses. Information from the Sloan Consortium reports that "over 4.6 million students were taking at least one online course during the fall 2008" (Allen and Seaman, 2010, p. 1). An article in *Campus Technology* shared research conducted by Ambient Insight, reporting that there are currently more than twelve million college students engaged in some form of online learning, with projections expecting this number to grow to more than twenty-two million postsecondary students by the year 2014 (Nagel, 2009). If even a fraction of those projections come true, faculty in higher education are going to have to become much more familiar with what technology is available to them and how they might use it to their instructional advantage.

For those of you not currently teaching online or in blended classroom environments, this book serves as a way of enhancing your onground classroom organization and instruction. The advantage of introducing these tools in onground classrooms, even pre-K through grade 12, is that you and your students will be better equipped to handle the learning curve when teaching or taking more tool-driven courses.

The First Webs

What Web are we on (and who cares)? No discussion of educational technology seems to get by without mention of Web 2.0. What difference does the number make in the process of teaching and learning? This is where our old stories come back into play.

The faculty who first began to interact with the Internet were the leading scientists and engineers of the 1960s and 1970s. You had to be a brilliant computer scientist to use very primitive list servers, e-mail protocols, and so forth in order to send or receive information. The general public wasn't online until the early to mid-1990s, when such subscription services as AOL and CompuServe came into existence. Surfing the Web was limited to whatever pages those services wanted to provide to the public. Very quickly, however, Web authoring tools made it possible for the average computer user (or instructor) to author his or her own content and make it available on the Internet. That was the birth of Web 1.0.

A decade later, Web 1.0 is described as the static Internet. Web pages were authored and offered for viewing, but there was little else a reader could do. An individual could bookmark a favorite page for later reference but could not make comments, tag or label the content, or very easily add to that information. In fact, that shift from reading as a consumer to contributing as a producer is one of the defining characteristics of Web 2.0.

Jones (2006) contends that self-expression has always been one of the primary uses for the Web, and offers blog growth to illustrate how the masses have employed technology for this purpose. He reports that in 1997 there were one hundred blogs on the Web site Xanga; by 2005 there were fifty million blogs. When the public learned that they could use the Internet to instantly share their ideas and resources, additional tools began to crop up, such those for sharing music, photos, and other files. Soon it was not enough to offer resources; users wanted to comment on one another's work, "tag" work with descriptive labels, and generally interact with what they were seeing online. Users moved from consuming what was available on the Internet to producing the content on the Internet. In 1993 you may have been able to look at someone's vacation photos. In 2010 you can search for photos using tags, find one and leave a comment for the photographer, download one that comes with a creative common license for reuse, and use it on your personal blog with permissions. The next reader can comment on your work, and so the cycle continues. Hence, "the value of the page is derived from the actions of users" (Elgan, 2006, para. 5).

Clay Shirky, a popular icon in defining and explaining the value of Web 2.0, specifically studies social media. His many presentations reinforce this idea of not only consuming Web media but also producing it. In a 2009 address on the *TED Blog* (Shirky, 2009), Shirky reminds us, "Every time a new consumer joins this media landscape, a new *producer* joins as well, because the same equipment, phones, computer lets you consume and produce." Harnessed as an educational tool, technology affords new possibilities for learners of all ages.

The technologies of Web 2.0 have been shaped with the idea of community. Alexander (2006, para. 14) adds that "the desire to discover, publish, and share appears far back in Internet history." Scholarship is predicated on the idea of having one's ideas debated, critiqued, and retooled by colleagues. This same spirit describes the rise of community-oriented technology tools in Web 2.0. These tools fit nicely with the belief that the meaning-making process of learning requires social interaction (Brown & Adler, 2008). From the practice of commenting on blogs to the ability to search within another scholar's bookmarks through social bookmarking sites, Web 2.0 technologies allow us to share and pool resources.

This openness and willingness to share come with a cost: it takes more time to follow the trail of information and ideas. The most significant development for managing time and resources has been rich site summary or Really Simple Syndication (RSS). Simply stated, RSS allows a user to follow information through subscription to the site. It is particularly helpful for organizing content that is updated—routinely or less predictably (Bell, 2009). Every time the content is updated, a notice is delivered to the user. The content could be a blog post, a podcast, or an announcement. That notice includes a title of the new content, metadata describing it, and a hyperlink to find the updated site. By using an RSS aggregator, a subscriber can also have the actual media downloaded automatically. Therefore, by subscribing to a site, the user always knows when new content is added.

RSS also helps authors and developers share their content with consumers more efficiently. By making one's blog posts, podcasts, or other media subscribable through an RSS feed, the author can develop a loyal following. This process of syndication is sometimes called a "pulling technology" (Bell, 2009) because it pulls readers or listeners back to the site repeatedly. No one seems to agree on exactly who should take credit for inventing RSS, but most of us recognize that it saves time and aggravation in trying to keep up with news and changes. Having the ability to author or interact with sites, and to keep up with those many changes through RSS, begins to round out our picture of what Web 2.0 means.

RSS has further helped define Web 2.0 by making those small pieces of content more important than the whole. Alexander (2006) describes these as microcontent, which includes blog posts or new podcasts. When a reader accesses the blog, for example, he or she does not read from start to finish as one might read a book. The reader instead focuses on the latest entry, the one piece of microcontent that may define whether he or she returns or subscribes. Similarly, a reader or fan may not agree with everything a blog author writes, but it may be that one post from January 2008 that gets bookmarked and used later for an academic paper.

No one quite knows when we transitioned to Web 2.0, but the move makes it possible for the average instructor to start using technologies to improve teaching and learning. Jones (2006, p. 5) writes, "One of the key factors in the Web 2.0 movement is technology. As Web developers master emerging tech such as Ajax, Web sites can implement a wide array of new feature sets that increase users' access and capabilities, which in turn allows them to create more original content for the Web." As Alexander (2006) noted, it is less important to define Web 2.0 precisely and more important to consider how the changes can influence education through projects and practices. Hargadon (2008) goes so far as to suggest that the development of Web 2.0 technologies and pedagogies will have a more significant impact than the printing press.

Our Future

The developments of the past five to ten years situate us nicely to continue with emerging technologies. Will there be a Web 3.0? Undoubtedly! However, it will probably not come crashing in on us, but will develop as quietly as Web 2.0 did. This time, it may not be consumers who drive the changes, but technologies themselves. Web 3.0 "will be about semantic web (or the meaning of data), personalization (e.g., iGoogle), [and] intelligent search and behavioral advertising among other things" (Agarwal, 2009, p. 1). It will be defined by the ability to manage copious amounts of data, which will require additional technological developments. Those technologies are probably already in place; we just are underutilizing their powers (Downes, 2009b).

To follow the development of future technologies from an expert's position, we can read the work of Kevin Kelly. Kelly's published predictions from 1997 have spurred a book on the topic of the future, *What Technology Wants* (2010), with significant parts written from the public's point of view. For example, Kelly (2009, para. 3) blogged, "The procession of technological discoveries is inevitable. When the conditions are right—when the necessary web of supporting technology needed for every invention is established—then the next adjacent technological step will emerge as if on cue." This next step will only be possible because of Web 2.0, not the older version.

The rise of Web 2.0, the coming of the next Web, and the inherent changes in how we consume and produce Web-based resources are driving an important time in teaching and learning. How we take these technologies and use them to our advantage is one of the great challenges for today's educators. It is that combination of technologies and instructional design that will set us apart. In Chapter Two we begin to look at how we can make informed decisions about the available tools.

CHAPTER TWO

HOW TO CHOOSE TOOLS AND A MATRIX FOR DOING SO

In Chapter One we explored the history of Web-based tools and how tools and Internet programs developed over time. Now we turn to a more specific focus: how to make technology tools work for your teaching situation. This chapter begins with a discussion about the relationship between instructional technology and instructional design. Based on the notion that technology tools should solve specific problems, we present a matrix for helping you choose the right tool for each one along with a full discussion about factors that should be considered such as accessibility and technical requirements.

Instructional Technology and Instructional Design

Instructional technology dates as far back as the printing press, which allowed the same information to be shared with multiple students simultaneously (Saettler, 2004). Even today, the term *technology* often refers to the tools that are used to assist in the delivery of a curriculum. However, in the late eighteenth and early nineteenth centuries, Johann Friedrich Herbart introduced technology as a *systematic* approach to instruction (Saettler). As Saettler noted, in 1970 the Commission on Instructional Technology defined instructional technology as "a systematic way of designing, carrying out, and evaluating the total process of learning and teaching in terms of specific objectives, based on research in human learning and communication, and employing a combination of human and nonhuman resources to bring about more effective instruction" (p. 6). Since this time, the definition has evolved. The Association for Educational Communications and Technology (2001) currently defines instructional technology as "the theory and practice of design, development, utilization, management, and evaluation of processes and resources for learning."

It is the combination of those human and nonhuman resources that makes for exciting instruction supported by instructional technology. But how do we make the connection? It is through the intentional and systematic application of instructional design that we combine the human and nonhuman resources to achieve instructional results.

Here is the central premise of our handbook: *technology tools must be used in the context of instructional design.* In other words, you must match your tool to your pedagogy. Before we go any further, let us demystify the word *pedagogy*. In this context, we are talking about instructional strategies or how one goes about teaching. If you want students to learn the vocabulary of your field, do you have them play games with the words, or use the words in sentences, or write short papers putting the words into context? Any of those three strategies could be labeled as pedagogy. You probably recognize that those three strategies are markedly different in terms of the complexity of cognitive ability that goes into the tasks, but they are nevertheless different pedagogies to achieve similar goals.

For the most part, teachers are subject-matter experts, not instructional designers. We are, after all, hired primarily as content experts, having studied and earned advanced degrees in political science, geology, or calculus, for example. What training we may have received in the art and science of instruction is secondary to our knowledge of the subject matter. Consequently, we do not usually follow a formal method for organizing instruction.

That said, most of us follow an intuitive model of organizing instruction. We rely on informal or tacit models, past experience, and common sense. Most of us begin each new lesson with a terminal objective, the idea or skill that must be mastered by the learner. We may create our terminal objectives or have a sense of what needs to be mastered by experience, but textbook publishers often provide this information as well.

There are a plethora of instructional design models, and it is beyond the scope of this book to explore them all. However, it is worthwhile to examine a few of the well-known models to seek similar themes and processes.

Selected Instructional Design Models

In this next section we review several of the most commonly used instructional design models. This is a not a comprehensive list of models, nor do we explore in depth any one model. However, for the reader, it is important to think about the process of planning instruction so that tool selection meets an instructional need. These models help us do that.

ADDIE

Perhaps the most readily identifiable instructional design model is the ADDIE model, although there is some debate as to whether this is an official model or an amalgam of other systems approaches (Morrison, Ross, & Kemp, 2007). The model follows a fairly linear approach: **A**nalyze, **D**esign, **D**evelop, **I**mplement, **E**valuate. It is during this first step of analysis that the instructional designer determines who the learners are, what knowledge gaps exist, and what it is that they need to learn. In other words, instructional objectives are crafted. During the remaining steps in instructional design, the designer determines how it is he or she will meet those objectives through developing activities that engage the learner, instructional materials and media to communicate the message, and methods for assessing learning and evaluating instruction. Figure 2.1 shows the major steps in the ADDIE model.

Instruction Aligned with Objectives

Mager (1988) proposes a model for instructional design that begins with goal or task analysis (what is to be learned), and then moves to specifying the instructional objectives and performance statement. In writing the performance statement, the designer precisely describes the behavior that will be observed and the context of where it will be performed. Further, the designer articulates the manner in which

FIGURE 2.1. MAJOR STEPS IN THE ADDIE MODEL

the behavior will be measured. This guides the designer in determining instructional strategies to bring about the desired change in performance or behavior.

What sets Mager's work apart from others' is the precision with which he develops instructional objectives. Beginning with a basic and sometimes vague instructional goal, he works through a process of naming behaviors that represent desired outcomes, and sorts them in terms of performance. The result is a precise declaration that if the learner should demonstrate the ultimate behavior, the instructor will know that subject matter was learned. This is done at a painstakingly detailed level, and may be more tedious than the process toward which the average instructor is inclined. Ultimately, Mager works toward asking the question, if a learner did what you proposed, would you be willing to say that he or she has mastered that objective? (Mager, 1988). For example, if a student correctly uses a vocabulary word, such as *cytoplasm*, *Golgi apparatus*, or *mitochondrion*, as he identifies cell parts, you would say he understands the structure of the cell. Further, if he adds cellular respiration to the mix, he probably is knowledgeable about function.

Following the articulation of instructional objectives, Mager goes on to plan for possible instructional strategies. He writes, "Without objectives, it is difficult to organize student efforts and activities for accomplishment of instructional intent" (Mager, 1975, p. 6). Here we begin to see the relationship between the objectives and the strategy: the wrong strategy will not yield the desired outcomes in terms of performance or behavior.

Dick, Carey, and Carey

The model presented by Dick, Carey, and Carey (2001) likewise begins with an analysis of broad curricular goals, the learners, and the context in which instruction is to occur. The authors give careful consideration to the learners and what skills they bring to the instructional setting, as well as other characteristics that may influence how readily they achieve success. When working with technology tools, a student's "readiness" with regard to technology significantly influences how he or she approaches tasks requiring tools.

Similar to Mager's work, the model of Dick, Carey, and Carey precisely delineates broad instructional goals as performance objectives. That is to say, each behavior or intended outcome is described in detail and is criterion referenced so that assessment is directly related to learning tasks.

The Dick, Carey, and Carey model also shares characteristics with ADDIE. The front end of the model begins with a detailed analysis of the context and instruction, moving to articulating objectives and then on to selecting strategies and developing materials. However, the model is iterative, in that steps may be repeated and clarified.

Morrison, Ross, and Kemp

Morrison, Ross, and Kemp (2007) present their own model of instructional design. This model begins with an overarching analysis of the problem to be solved. In that context, the analysis must reveal that instruction is the best way to solve whatever problem the individual or organization faces. Assuming instruction is the solution, the model is framed by four basic questions:

1. Who is the learner (including his or her needs and characteristics)?
2. What do you want the learner to learn or demonstrate (objectives)?
3. How is that skill or content best learned (instructional strategies)?
4. How will you know when learning is achieved (assessment and evaluation)?

Although the Morrison, Ross, and Kemp framework is not presented as a linear model but rather as an iterative, cyclical model, there are many similarities between it and ADDIE. Hanley (2010) juxtaposed ADDIE onto the Morrison, Ross, and Kemp model, noting the areas that address ADDIE elements (see Figure 2.2). The selection of instructional strategies and the ultimate assessment

FIGURE 2.2. ADDIE JUXTAPOSED ONTO THE MORRISON, ROSS, AND KEMP MODEL

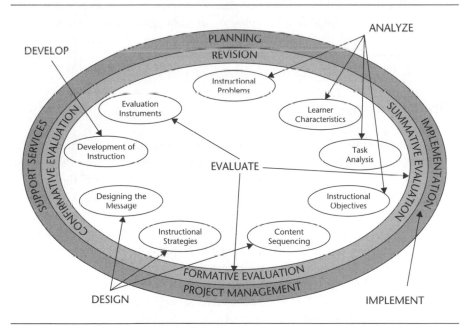

Source: Hanley (2010). Used by permission.

methods are entirely dependent on who the learner is and what it is you want the learner to know or demonstrate.

Matching Tools to Pedagogy

The models we reviewed have several elements in common: (1) a need to know the learners, their capabilities, and their attitudes; (2) a problem to solve or precise instructional objectives; and (3) the belief that instruction will address the problem or objectives. But how do we make decisions concerning which technology tools will help us achieve the desired outcomes?

Robert Reiser (2001), in his article "A History of Instructional Design and Technology. Part 1: A History of Instructional Media," writes: "Professionals in the field of instructional design and technology often use systematic instructional design procedures and employ a variety of instructional media to accomplish their goals. Moreover, in recent years, they have paid increasing attention to non-instructional solutions to some performance problems" (p. 53).

When we solve problems using technology tools, we begin to match the tools to our pedagogy. Teachers have done this for centuries. If you wanted to teach a student to read, for example, you would have to provide text (the tool). If you wanted the learner to differentiate between baroque and impressionist music, you would play samples on the phonograph (the tool). In the twenty-first century, our tools have changed, but ideally not the practice of matching tools to pedagogy.

What to Consider

Before introducing the Decision-Making Matrix and its categories, we should examine a few broad considerations. These will not only help us match our tool choice to our pedagogy but also help us focus on the other important components that affect what tool we choose. For example, you may decide that video conferencing is the best tool to help students feel connected within your virtual classroom (Moore, 1993). However, cost can be a major contributing factor, depending on the video conferencing tool you choose. In other words, we must take multiple components into consideration when choosing a tool, keeping in mind that meeting our course goals and objectives are the primary concerns. What follows is a list of considerations to keep in mind when choosing a teaching tool, which ultimately form our Decision-Making Matrix.

Problem It Solves

The selection of a tool should involve a complex decision-making process. Otherwise, you may select a tool that creates a problem instead of addressing a need. Some of the considerations include accessibility, learner readiness or characteristics, as well as such technical concerns as bandwidth available to users. The instructional problem should be determined in some kind of analysis phase of your instructional design process.

Platform: Online or Traditional?

In many cases, our examples relate to teaching online. That is, after all, where technology tools are required. However, many of these tools are also applicable to traditional instruction or the blended classroom. As we work through the examples in this handbook, we will attempt to point out where tools can be especially helpful in traditional or blended classrooms. When no Web-based application is available, we also identify if the product is Windows or Mac based.

Best Used For

You must evaluate how well the tool you are considering helps you meet the stated goals and objectives of the course based on your instructional design. These goals and objectives are what drive all curriculum decisions. To do this, you need an understanding of the instructional design process—specifically the creation of measurable goals and objectives.

Cost

It's important to evaluate the cost to the institution or students of using a specific tool. Although there are many free or inexpensive tools out there, sometimes the cost of commercial tools can be justified if they solve problems that require large amounts of staff time or other resources that result in monetary expenditure.

Accessibility

The accessibility of the technology tool is a component important to student success. In examining accessibility, you should begin planning the necessary steps to ensure that the content shared using the technology tool is accessible to persons with multiple learning needs and technical competencies. For example, if you decide that PowerPoint slides are the best tool for sharing specific information, you must ask how accessible the slides themselves are for students to access and review. If students will be using the tool to create content or interact, then you must also evaluate how accessible the tool is to use. For example, if you ask students to create a collaborative document and decide that they must use a specific wiki to do this, you might ask how easy is it for someone who uses a screen reader. A screen reader is a device that allows a visually impaired user to listen to text that would appear on a computer screen. In other words, it takes a web page or document and "reads" it into the ear of the user. Being effective at evaluating this criterion requires you to have a basic understanding of accessibility issues as they relate to the use of Web-based tools and services.

Special Equipment (Technical Requirements)

Technical requirements comprise the list of hardware and software requirements needed to use the technology tool. It's important to understand whether the requirements are standard to most computer users and whether or not they correspond with the advertised requirements of your course or program. For example, students who are told during the registration process that they do not need microphones should not all of a sudden be expected to have or purchase them. Assessing this criterion requires a basic understanding both of computer hardware and of your learner profiles created during the instructional design process.

Level of Expertise

Technical competencies are the skills needed in order to use the technology tool or service you plan to implement. Evaluating technical competencies requires an understanding of your learner profiles and the average skills with which learners will arrive. You analyze these skills during the instructional design process based on precourse surveys, past experience, and other analysis tools. You can also evaluate the skills your students currently have based on their experience in your course. However, once your course begins, it can be very time-consuming to help students learn the basic technical competencies needed to be successful in your course. The more you know about their technical abilities before class begins, the better you can prepare by creating tutorials, providing examples, and identifying additional resources from which students can get needed help. When evaluating a new tool, you will want to compare the technical competencies needed to use that tool with the technical competencies of your students before deciding on whether or not to use it.

Synchronous Versus Asynchronous

When evaluating a tool, it is important to know whether it requires asynchronous or synchronous communication. A synchronous tool allows you to communicate in real time; telephones, chat rooms, and instant messaging are examples. An asynchronous tool is used to send a message that may not be received immediately; e-mail and discussion forums are the best known examples. Using synchronous tools is a great way to meet with students individually or privately, provide students with the ability to present content to peers, and reduce the transactional distance between you and your students (Moore, 1993). However, synchronous tools can also be more difficult to plan for, and they require that students understand the place and time requirements sometimes unfamiliar to online learners.

Vocabulary

You may find that with new technology tools come new terms and lingo. Not only will you be required to learn these terms, but also you will need to be able to define them for your students in relation to your support materials and course content. Evaluating the number of new terms students must learn to understand and use a tool can also help you better determine whether or not there is sufficient time to introduce the tool to students in a manner that encourages their successful use of the tool.

Selection Matrix for Choosing the Right Tool

Using these categories, we have created a Decision-Making Matrix that organizes a summary of the above information. The matrix helps you quickly compare technology tools and share your findings with administrative staff or other instructors when necessary.

How to Use the Decision-Making Matrix

The Decision-Making Matrix is easy to use, and it is set up so that all you have to do is fill in the blanks. However, this assumes that you understand the underlying components that complement each section of the matrix. Therefore, we have created a supplemental guide in Table 2.2 with extensive information and resources to help you answer the questions on the matrix. After using both documents for a while, it is likely that you will be able to fill in the blanks on the matrix without looking at the supplemental guide.

Let's walk through the process of using the matrix. As you are developing a course or program through a systematic instructional design process, you may find yourself wondering how your students might meet a specific instructional goal. For example, in a human resources course, you may want your students to work in groups to collaborate on the creation of a policy manual. You might identify a problem of how students will be able to efficiently work on the same document at the same time. As a result, you may conduct research on free wiki tools that are available on the net. Wikis are Web-based tools that allow users to invite others to create documents together collaboratively. You would then use the matrix to evaluate each wiki or similar tool to determine which is best for you. Table 2.1 is a matrix completed after reviewing Google Docs, a free wiki-like tool offered by Google.

Key Concepts You Should Know

The Decision-Making Matrix is a great tool if you are already familiar with instructional design, accessibility, and technical information. However, we don't expect everybody to be an expert in all these categories. We have thus created a supplementary resource to help you ask the important questions necessary to complete the matrix in a more educated manner (see Table 2.2). This resource is in the form of a rating scale based on criteria in the areas of Course Goals and Objectives, Accessibility, Technical Requirements, and Reliability, which are explained below. Each of the categories could justify a book of its own. As a matter of fact, most of these topics have several books dedicated to them. Here we provide a brief description of each category and a list of resources from which you can learn more if needed.

Course Goals and Objectives. In this section you evaluate how well the tool you are considering helps you meet the stated goals and objectives of the course, based on your instructional design process. These are what drive all curriculum decisions. This section requires an understanding of the instructional design process, specifically the creation of measurable goals and objectives. If you'd like to learn more about this topic, consider these resources:

Dick, W., Carey, L., & Carey, J. (2008). *The systematic design of instruction* (7th ed.). Boston: Allyn & Bacon.

Gagné, R. M., Wager, W. W., Golas, K. C., & Keller, J. M. (2005). *Principles of instructional design* (5th ed.). Beverly, MA: Wadsworth.

Morrison, G. R., Ross, S. M., & Kemp, J. E. (2007). *Designing effective instruction* (5th ed.). New York: Wiley.

Accessibility. In this section you evaluate how accessible the technology tool is and begin planning the necessary steps to ensure the content shared using this technology is accessible to persons with multiple learning needs and different

TABLE 2.1. DECISION-MAKING MATRIX—GOOGLE DOCS

	Google Docs
Type of Tool	Organization communication and collaboration
Problem It Solves	This product solves the problem of how to get students to collaborate on one document when they are separated by distance. They can all access the document, add to it, or edit. The instructor can monitor progress.
Cost	Free
URL	http://docs.google.com/
Description	Users share documents, spreadsheets, presentations, and Web forms instantly and collaborate in real time or save the work for someone to review later. Users pick exactly who can access their documents, and can edit documents from anywhere. There is nothing to download—a browser is all that is needed.
Platform	Web
Best Used For	Multiple people collaborating on a single document
Level of Expertise	*Teacher:* Intermediate *Student:* Basic
Cautions	In order to edit a document, each user must have a free Google Account, and there is a first-time log-in. It may be necessary to help students establish their accounts.
Overcoming Cautions	The instructor should demonstrate the tool's use in the classroom or in a live Web-conferencing session. The instructor initiates the process by creating groups and documents, and invites students to collaborate to help facilitate organization.
Accessibility Concerns	There are issues of access and use for those who use screen readers. However, instructions for using Google Docs with a screen reader are available.
Special Equipment	None
Additional Vocabulary	*Wiki*
Training and Resources	www.google.com/google-d-s/intl/en/tour1.html http://docs.google.com/support/bin/answer.py?hl—en&answer=152439

technical competencies. This section requires you to have a basic understanding of accessibility issues as they relate to the use of Web-based tools and services. If you'd like to learn more about this topic, consider these resources:

- Electronic and Information Technology Accessibility Standards (Section 508) at www.access-board.gov/sec508/standards.htm
- Illinois Information Technology Accessibility Act at www.dhs.state.il.us/page.aspx?item=32765
- Implementation Guidelines for Web-Based Information and Applications 1.0 at www.dhs.state.il.us/IITAA/IITAAWebImplementationGuidelines.html
- Universal Design for Learning at www.cast.org/index.html
- W3C at www.w3.org/
- Web Content Accessibility Guidelines (WCAG) 2.0 at www.w3.org/TR/WCAG/

Technical Requirements. In this section you evaluate the hardware and software requirements of the technology tool to help determine whether the requirements are standard to most computer users. This section requires a basic understanding of computer hardware and of your learner profiles formed during the instructional design process. If you'd like to learn more about this topic, consider the following resource:

> Shelly, G. B., Cashman, T. J., & Vermaat, M. E. (2008). *Essential introduction to computers: And how to purchase a personal computer* (7th ed.). Boston: Thomson Course Technology.

Technical Competencies. In this section you evaluate the skills needed in order to use the technology tool or service you hope to implement. This section requires an understanding of your learner profiles and the average skills with which students will arrive, analyzed during the instructional design process; and the skills they currently have, based on their experience in your course. If you'd like to learn more about this topic, consider this resource:

> Levine, J. R., & Levine Young, M. (2010). *The Internet for dummies* (12th ed.). Indianapolis: Wiley.

Reliability. In this section you evaluate the tool's overall reliability in regard to functionality, longevity, and availability and downtime. This section requires research into the company that operates and maintains the tool and current user comments and ratings, along with a general sense of trends within the field of

TABLE 2.2. SUPPLEMENTAL GUIDE

Category	Criteria	Rating
Course Goals and Objectives	The tool helps meet goals and objectives.	☐ Yes ☐ Possibly ☐ No
Accessibility	The tool follows general standards for accessibility, such as those outlined in Section 508 of the Electronic and Information Technology Accessibility Standards, W3C, or the Web Content Accessibility Guidelines (WCAG)	☐ Yes ☐ Possibly ☐ No
	The tool is easy to access and to install if necessary.	☐ Yes ☐ Possibly ⊔ No
	Video content has closed-captioning, or a transcript is available.	☐ Yes ☐ Possibly ☐ No
	A transcript accompanies audio content.	☐ Yes ☐ Possibly ☐ No
	The tool and its content can be easily manipulated to accommodate users with special needs.	☐ Yes ☐ Possibly ☐ No
Technical Requirements	The tool can be accessed and used by multiple operating systems, such as Windows- and Mac-based machines.	☐ Yes ☐ Possibly ☐ No
	The tool requires no additional hardware or software beyond that already expected of students enrolled in the course.	☐ Yes ☐ Possibly ☐ No
	The tool requires few to no additional skills beyond those already expected of students in the course.	☐ Yes ☐ Possibly ☐ No
	Additional support materials are available or can easily be created to help students learn how to use the tool in regard to meeting the needs of the course.	☐ Yes ☐ Possibly ☐ No
Reliability	The company that operates and maintains the tool has been in existence for a while and has proven stability within the field.	☐ Yes ☐ Possibly ☐ No
	The tool has been in existence long enough to be tested such that it is not considered to be in beta form.	☐ Yes ☐ Possibly ☐ No
	User and tester comments and ratings suggest the tool is of high quality.	☐ Yes ☐ Possibly ☐ No

educational technology. If you'd like to learn more about this topic, consider these resources:

Evaluating Internet research sources. Retrieved from www.virtualsalt.com/evalu8it.htm

Harris, R. (2007, June 15). *Evaluating internet research sources*. Retrieved from http://www.virtualsalt.com/evalu8it.htm

Evaluating Internet sources. Retrieved from www.library.illinois.edu/ugl/howdoi/webeval.html

Avery, S. (2009, August 7). *Evaluating internet sources*. Retrieved from http://www.library.illinois.edu/ugl/howdoi/webeval.html

Too Many Tools Is a Problem!

As much as we love technology tools, we would also like to remind you that it has been our experience that requiring students to use too many tools within one class can become overwhelming and frustrating, and can distract students from meeting instructional goals. Therefore, keep the number of tools to a minimum. We suggest no more than two or three new tools within a single term, unless you know you are working with an experienced cohort.

As we face the challenges of a growing population, global classrooms, and distant students, we will be required to be more inventive in our delivery methods. As mentioned earlier in this chapter, no matter what tool you use, it should always solve an instructional problem identified in your instructional design process. As technology tools change, your ability to evaluate them and their academic effectiveness should not waiver. Our hope is that the matrix we developed will provide you with a lifelong process for evaluating new tools as they emerge.

A Word About Safety

For teachers who work with children in grades K through 12, the child's privacy must be of foremost concern when selecting tools. We are confident you are familiar with your school's policies and procedures, but this is a good place to remind you of some basic practices you may want to investigate. Companies who specifically direct their services to children under the age of thirteen must follow the provisions of the Children's Online Privacy Protection Act

(COPPA) and should state this in their information. For example, TweenTribune (a news digest and blogging tool for "tween-age" children) states that it is in compliance with COPPA and gives specifics about its policies and procedures on its information page. Look for this kind of safety endorsement as you consider tools for young users.

PART TWO

TOOLS TO HELP YOU STAY ORGANIZED

Now that we have a foundational understanding of how to approach decision making when incorporating tools, we can focus on technologies that help us solve problems. In that framework of problem solving, Part Two focuses on Web-based tools instructors can use to help them organize their time, ideas, and resources.

The stereotype of the absent-minded professor may have come from those who, despite their obvious intelligence and subject-matter expertise, sometimes frustrate us due to their lack of organizational skills. This lack contributes to missed meetings, lost student papers, and more. We have all seen our offices inundated with final papers at the end of the term along with committee reports and agendas for upcoming projects. And truthfully, it seems that the rate of change has accelerated to the point where we all need a little help keeping on top of our responsibilities, not to mention the paperwork or the digital files.

The tools we discuss in this section can be used in the design, development, and implementation stages of the instructional design process. These include calendars, scheduling aids, mind-mapping or graphic organizer tools, social bookmarking, and virtual file management or storage. Although most instructors are familiar with the idea of maintaining a calendar or a filing system, they may not be familiar with the idiosyncrasies and functionality offered via Web-based tools. Furthermore, many of these tools can aid students in staying on task and managing resources and materials as they work independently and in groups.

CHAPTER THREE

CALENDARS

If someone caught you on the street and asked what you were doing next Tuesday at one o'clock, how would you answer? Would you tell him you need to get back to him after you consult your paper calendar, would you look it up on your smartphone, or would you have it committed to memory? This chapter introduces Web-based calendar systems that allow you to organize your time and decide what details to share with students, parents, or the general public. We look at the nature of calendar tools by answering a set of general questions, which we follow with an example of our Decision-Making Matrix completed for the two products.

What Is the Tool?

A calendar can be used to record your schedule, such as when you have classes to teach or meetings to attend. It can also be used as a tool to communicate due dates and deadlines for students if you construct calendars for individual classes. Most course management systems have calendars built into them for online classes, but the tools we examine are independent products that allow you to manage and integrate multiple calendars using a single interface. These tools also enable you to assign roles and permissions to students that allow them to either view calendar events or add their own.

What Problem Does It Solve?

A calendar keeps you organized and on schedule. By looking at where deadlines intersect, you can better manage your workload; you can avoid having three sections of classes turning in lab reports on the same day. For students, a calendar helps keep them from missing deadlines.

Is This Something Instructors or Students Use?

Both instructors and students use calendars. Typically the instructor initiates a calendar and shares the online version with students. In turn, students can synchronize their own schedules and exercise good study and time management skills. You can make a calendar more interactive if you include hyperlinks to course materials or resources.

Is This Tool for the Novice, Intermediate, or Expert?

This is a tool a novice can use.

Is There Special Equipment or Software Needed?

No special equipment or software is needed. You only need a Web browser.

What Are Some Cautions About This Tool?

The main concern with this tool is privacy. What you put online is available for everyone to see. If you manage several calendars, including a personal version and a class calendar, you need to be careful about the information to which your students have access. You may not want them to know your daughter has an oboe lesson next Monday. Calendaring tools allow you to control what is public and what is not, but be sure to read the instructions carefully.

How Accessible Is This Tool to All Users?

Persons who use screen readers may have trouble with Web-based calendars. Because a calendar is visual and set up with tables and pop-ups, the individual using a screen reader must address a good deal of coding detail to successfully navigate the site. Both Google Calendar and 30 Boxes also fail the test of having pages that can be accessed with either a keyboard or a mouse (they require a pointing device). That makes the tool less friendly for those with mobility problems, too.

What Additional Vocabulary Do I Need to Know?

You don't need any additional vocabulary.

Can You Share a K–12 Example?

Imagine you are teaching five classes a day, supervising a student teacher, sitting on your department's curriculum committee, and coaching the school's tennis team. As you can see, there are a lot of dates and times to manage. For example, you have the assignment due dates for each of your five classes, test dates, parent-teacher conferences, department meetings, school events, tennis matches, and meetings with your student teacher. This doesn't include the outside calendar events you may have that involve your family or volunteer interests. In this situation, a Web-based calendaring tool could allow you to create a calendar for each of your courses and then a personal calendar for all other events. By doing this, you can provide your parents and students with a link to see when assignments are due or what dates tests will be on. Your personal calendar can include your meeting dates and times and be restricted to your viewing only. As the administrator of the account, you can see all events from all calendars on a single Web page, allowing you to refrain from double-booking or overloading yourself by accidentally having multiple large assignments from multiple classes falling due at the same time—and during the tennis tournament, of all times. Figure 3.1 shows what this schedule may look like from the administrator's viewpoint.

Can You Share a Higher Education Example?

Imagine you are teaching three classes (all requiring group project work), writing a research article for a major publication journal in your field, and overseeing the student-teaching course. Your work schedule may include course assignment deadlines, individual and group meetings with students, benchmarks for your article, and on-site visits with your student teachers. A Web-based calendaring tool can help you create a calendar for each one of your classes; a calendar for your student-teaching program; and a calendar for your more personal events, such as the draft and final submission dates for your article. To make your calendar more interactive, you can allow your students to add events to their classes' calendars, including the dates and times of group meetings they are conducting outside of the classroom. This helps you get a picture of how often your students are meeting to work on their group projects for your classes. Having this information

FIGURE 3.1. SAMPLE CALENDAR CREATED USING GOOGLE CALENDAR

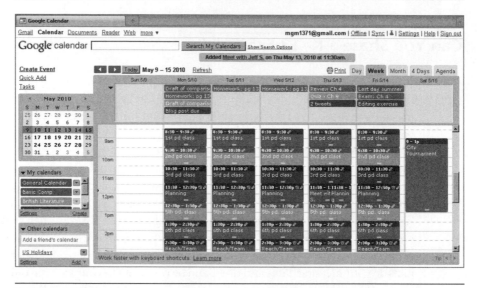

Used by permission.

FIGURE 3.2. SAMPLE CALENDAR CREATED USING 30 BOXES

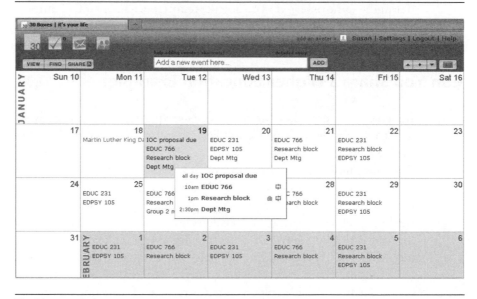

Used by permission.

also gives you the opportunity to attend these meetings if desired, which is particularly easy if the meetings are held in a virtual environment, for example using Web conferencing (see Chapter Fourteen). As the calendar administrator, you will be able to see your entire schedule in one view. You can also view only one calendar at a time when needed. Figure 3.2 shows an example of what your complete calendar view may look like.

Where Can I Learn More?

In general, when you need support for an online tool, you look to the support pages for that tool. For example, Google Calendar's help is available at www.google.com/support/calendar/.

Currently Available Tools

- Google Calendar at www.google.com/calendar/
- 30 Boxes at http://30boxes.com/

TABLE 3.1. DECISION-MAKING MATRIX—CALENDARS

	Google Calendar	30 Boxes
Type of Tool	Organization communication and collaboration	Organization communication and collaboration
Problem It Solves	This tool gives instructors the ability to see and manage time and to communicate appropriate details to students. It keeps teachers and students on task.	This tool gives instructors the ability to see and manage time and to communicate appropriate details to students. It keeps teachers and students on task.
Cost	Free	Free
URL	http://calendar.google.com	http://30boxes.com/
Description	Google calendar is a visual representation of the old paper version. You can enter appointments, meetings, and classes, along with due dates and deadlines. You can also invite people to events through the calendar. You can share portions with others so they know when you're busy and when you're free. The calendar can be synchronized to smartphones so updates are portable.	30 Boxes is a Web-based visual representation of the old paper version. You can enter appointments, meetings, and classes, along with due dates and deadlines. You can also share portions with others so they know when you're busy and when you're free. Other users can also schedule appointments and add to your calendar. Finally, you can send reminders to yourself and others and connect to social media.

(continued)

TABLE 3.1. (*continued*)

	Google Calendar	30 Boxes
Platform	Web	Web
Best Used For	Maintaining a personal and class schedule that can be shared with others.	Maintaining a personal and class schedule that can be shared with others. Groups can plan and coordinate schedules.
Level of Expertise	*Teacher:* Basic *Student:* Basic	*Teacher:* Basic *Student:* Basic
Cautions	The user must have a free account with Google to establish a calendar. Those wishing to view your calendar do not need accounts unless they want to establish their own calendars and synchronize them with yours. The primary concern, however, is loss of privacy.	You must first establish an account. You need to set permissions to allow others to view and add to your calendar. The main concern, however, is loss of privacy.
Overcoming Cautions	To overcome the privacy issue, establish a personal calendar that you do not share with the public. Create a different calendar for individual class sections with important dates and deadlines.	To overcome the privacy issue, you can control the settings and the extent to which others can see your personal information.
Accessibility Concerns	The tool presents challenges for persons with visual impairment who use screen readers and for those with mobility difficulties, because it requires a pointing device and cannot be accessed with only a keyboard. In both cases, a simple, linear text listing of dates and deadlines would work better.	The tool presents challenges for persons with visual impairment who use screen readers and for those with mobility difficulties, because it requires a pointing device and cannot be accessed with only a keyboard. In both cases, a simple, linear text listing of dates and deadlines would work better. Pop-ups also present a problem with screen readers.
Special Equipment	None	None
Additional Vocabulary	None	None
Training and Resources	www.google.com/support/calendar/?hl=en	http://30boxes.com/help

CHAPTER FOUR

SCHEDULING TOOLS

On the off chance that you remember your schedule for the first Tuesday of next month, if someone wanted to meet with you at ten o'clock in the morning, would you be able to "pencil in" that appointment? What if you were not available and had to search for a time? That is where a Web-based scheduling tool can help. Such a tool allows other people to peruse your schedule, find mutually agreeable times, and schedule meetings. Those campuses that use Microsoft Office tools may have trained instructors to use the calendar and scheduling features in Outlook; however, not everyone has the full suite of Microsoft Office tools. Plus, those outside of your office who are not connected to your network still are unable to see your availability or add appointments to your calendar. The Web-based products we discuss in this chapter work with all users, regardless of e-mail clients or software they have installed on their personal computers, and in some cases can be synchronized with Outlook or other existing calendars.

What Is the Tool?

A scheduling tool allows you to make all or portions of your schedule available to the public so that they can schedule appointments with you. You determine how much of your schedule to share and control who sees it. For example, you could block off a window of time for students in one class to schedule phone appointments, and have colleagues in your faculty committee see a different block of time.

What Problem Does It Solve?

Scheduling tools solve the problem of finding mutually agreeable times for meeting without having the hassle of negotiating, which can be frustrating, especially if done over e-mail. By the time a date is set, you could have exchanged five to ten messages and wasted over an hour of time. Online scheduling tools allow the person who wants to meet with you to see your schedule and find a mutually agreeable time without directly communicating with you. Therefore, scheduling can occur at times when you would otherwise be unavailable for a conversation.

Furthermore, for scheduling group meetings, some of these tools allow members to see each other's schedules. Not to put pressure on one member, but if you see that four of the five members are available for a meeting at noon and your only obligation is lunch, you might reconsider for the good of the group (and tell everyone to brown-bag it). Or, if Sam is out of town for the meeting, this might indicate that the meeting needs to occur via phone and not in person.

Is This Something Instructors or Students Use?

Surely both instructors and students can use this tool. Usually an instructor would start the process by creating a schedule and asking students to make appointments. However, students could also use this tool to schedule group meetings with one another.

Is This Tool for the Novice, Intermediate, or Expert?

This is a tool a novice can use.

Is There Special Equipment or Software Needed?

No special equipment or software is needed. You only need a Web browser.

What Are Some Cautions About This Tool?

Aside from the fact that even the best technology cannot make others more available when you need them, the main caution with this tool pertains to privacy. Although you control who sees what is in your schedule, a little common sense is in order. We don't need to know you are unavailable on the 26th because you have a dentist appointment. In most cases, scheduling tools do not show anything more than blocks of time during which you are free or available. However, it's important to know what visitors see and how to set your privacy options within your chosen calendar tool. And there is always a chance someone else will find your schedule and make fictitious appointments. It's not likely, but it could happen with younger audiences.

How Accessible Is This Tool to All Users?

For the most part, these tools are accessible. In general, they do not use frames or tables, but when these are used they are labeled appropriately. The scripting is clean, and persons with visual impairments can use screen readers. The sites do not deal with multimedia and graphics. However, scheduling tools do require a mouse (pointing device), so persons with mobility problems could have difficulty.

What Additional Vocabulary Do I Need to Know?

You don't need any additional vocabulary.

Can You Share a K–12 Example?

The classic scheduling need for K–12 teachers pertains to parent-teacher conferences. They happen at least once a year and require several weeks' lead time to get appointments set. Let's imagine you teach second grade and need to meet with each of your twenty students' parents over a three-day span. In the past, you may have sent a note home and asked parents to respond with their available times. Chances are good that at least one of your most conscientious parents was late responding or lost the note. With a Web-based tool, you send a URL and ask parents to schedule directly during your available appointment times. They can do this at any time and request reminder e-mails. If a week before conferences you see that a parent has not responded, you can intervene quickly. Figure 4.1 shows what this schedule may look like from the parent's viewpoint.

Can You Share a Higher Education Example?

You have been appointed as the chair of the faculty technology usage group. Congratulations, you need to coordinate the schedules of eleven other members, including four adjunct instructors who do not access their calendars or e-mail on campus and two student representatives. This is the time to use a Web-based tool,

FIGURE 4.1. TIMEDRIVER SCHEDULING TOOL

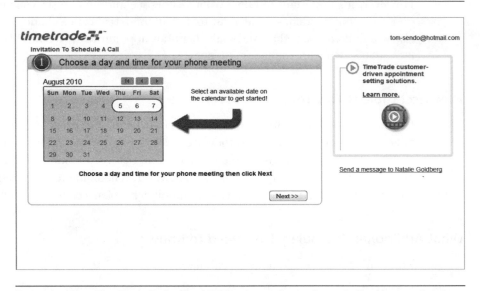

Screenshot from TimeTrade Professional Edition (www.timetrade.com). Used by permission.

FIGURE 4.2. SURVEY FOR TIME AVAILABILITY IN DOODLE

Doodle: Faculty Technology Usage G...														

"Please indicate your availability so we can schedule a meeting."

Time zone: America/Chicago ▼ Update

	January 2010														
	Mon 25				Tue 26				Wed 27				Thu 28		
	10:00 AM	12:00 PM	2:00 PM	4:00 PM	10:00 AM	12:00 PM	2:00 PM	4:00 PM	10:00 AM	12:00 PM	2:00 PM	4:00 PM	10:00 AM	12:00 PM	2:00 PM
Jane Kennedy		OK		OK		OK	OK		OK		OK				OK
Magello Ortiz		OK	OK		OK	OK					OK	OK	OK	OK	
Brita Miller	OK			OK		OK	OK		OK			OK		OK	OK
Tracy Jackson	OK	OK							OK	OK			OK	OK	
Chris Stein		OK	OK		OK	OK					OK	OK	OK	OK	
Kevin Johnson		OK	OK		OK	OK									
Susan Manning	☐	☐	☐	☐	☐	☐	☐	☐	☐	☐	☐	☐	☐	☐	☐
Count	2	5	3	2	3	4	2	1	2	2	2	4	3	4	2

Used by permission.

send the URL to members, and have them indicate their availability. With such a tool, you can isolate a block of dates and times when you would be available to meet, and then ask each member to signify his or her availability. You can set the parameters so that everyone in the group sees each other's responses. Quickly, you'll know where you might find the time for the meetings. Figure 4.2 shows what this schedule may look like from the administrator's viewpoint. In this case, it looks like only one person is unavailable on Monday at noon.

Where Can I Learn More?

In general, when you need support for an online tool, you look to the support pages for that tool. For example, Doodle's help is available at www.doodle.com/about/help.html.

Currently Available Tools

- Doodle at www.doodle.com
- TimeDriver at http://timedriver.timetrade.com

TABLE 4.1. DECISION-MAKING MATRIX—SCHEDULING TOOLS

	TimeDriver	Doodle
Type of Tool	Organization communication and collaboration	Organization communication and collaboration
Problem It Solves	This tool solves a scheduling problem. It allows people to schedule appointments with you, including group appointments.	This tool solves the problem of finding a common meeting time. It allows people to respond to surveys about time availability.
Cost	Inexpensive (free trial available)	Free
URL	http://timedriver.timetrade.com	www.doodle.com
Description	This is a Web-based tool that allows others to schedule appointments after checking your calendar. It synchronizes nicely with Google Calendar and Microsoft Outlook.	Doodle is a Web-based tool that allows others to state their availability so you can schedule meetings. It works like a survey.

(continued)

TABLE 4.1. (*continued*)

	TimeDriver	Doodle
Platform	Web	Web
Best Used For	Getting individuals to schedule appointments with you	Finding out about availability for groups of people
Level of Expertise	*Teacher:* Basic *Student:* Basic	*Teacher:* Basic *Student:* Basic
Cautions	The primary caution relates to privacy. You're letting others know about your availability.	If this tool is used with students, they can see each other's responses. Some may not like the openness of that.
Overcoming Cautions	It is possible to coordinate your existing calendar (for example, with Google Calendar or Outlook) with TimeDriver. Just be sure your calendar is up-to-date. Therefore, if you do not want people to know why you're busy, do not give details; just block out the time.	Remind students that they need to respect one another's privacy.
Accessibility Concerns	This tool is accessible to most populations, but may present challenges for those with mobility concerns because a pointing device (mouse) is required.	This tool is accessible to most populations, but may present challenges for those with mobility concerns because a pointing device (mouse) is required for polls.
Special Equipment	None	None
Additional Vocabulary	None	None
Training and Resources	http://timedriver.timetrade.com/support.php	www.doodle.com/about/help.html

CHAPTER FIVE

MIND-MAPPING OR GRAPHIC ORGANIZER TOOLS

You know that at times a picture is worth a thousand words. Remember ninth-grade English when your teacher asked you to outline your next essay? Not everyone can produce a classical outline, and it turns out that some of us think in pictures and organize our thoughts accordingly. There is a good deal of evidence that the use of graphic organizers helps students focus on the relationships between concepts more than on the words themselves. Whether the teacher or a publisher has prepared the organizer to support text, or whether or not the organizer is student generated, the user sees and interprets concepts that are organized spatially (McKenzie, 2003; Hall, Bailey, & Tillman, 1997). Other terms for graphic organizers include *knowledge maps, concepts maps, story maps, advanced organizers,* and more (Hall & Strangman, 2002). This chapter introduces you to the idea of using Web-based tools to help organize thoughts and ideas.

What Is the Tool?

A graphic organizer tool allows the user to draw a graphic representation of ideas, facts, or concepts and to show relationships spatially. As a Web-based process, the activity of organizing and classifying information often occurs online but is capable of being exported for use off-line.

What Problem Does It Solve?

Graphic organizers help students move beyond text-only readings and allow them to view or interpret concepts, facts, or ideas spatially. For students with different learning styles or for those with learning disabilities, this can be especially helpful (Hall & Strangman, 2002).

Is This Something Instructors or Students Use?

Faculty could use these tools to prepare in advance graphic organizers that interpret text or facts for student use. However, students could use these tools to generate their own representations of text or class content.

Is This Tool for the Novice, Intermediate, or Expert?

This is a tool a novice can use.

Is There Special Equipment or Software Needed?

No special equipment or software is needed. You only need a Web browser.

What Are Some Cautions About This Tool?

In most cases, the user needs to establish an account. Although accounts are often free, teachers with young students might want to generate institutional accounts to protect student privacy.

How Accessible Is This Tool to All Users?

For the most part, these tools are not accessible for those who use screen readers. By nature, they are graphic, and created content often involves small text sizes, various colors, and other features that present problems for those with visual impairments. Because the creation of the graphics often requires a mouse, those who only access the tool with keyboards may have difficulty as well.

What Additional Vocabulary Do I Need To Know?

Concept map—much the same as a mind map, a visual representation of ideas and their relationships

Graphic organizer—any tool for visually representing information

Knowledge map—same as a concept map, a visual representation of ideas and their relationships

K-W-L—an instructional method through which teachers ask students to organize what they know (K), what they want to know (W), and what they've learned (L) in a table

Mind map—an image that starts with a central idea and relates concepts, facts, and information through visual connections

Can You Share a K–12 Example?

You teach fifth grade and introduce your students to the idea of organizing a persuasive speech. Using Mindmeister, each student selects a topic and begins to think about the components that should be included in the speech. One student's work partway through the process is represented in Figure 5.1. Later, as you review the progress this student made in organizing her ideas, you can suggest additional research she could include to strengthen her argument.

FIGURE 5.1. GRAPHIC ORGANIZER CREATED WITH WEBSPIRATION

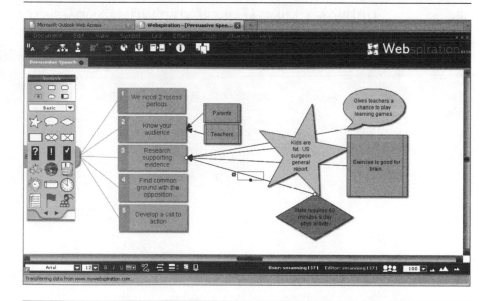

Diagram created in Webspiration™ by Inspiration® Software Inc. Used by permission.

Can You Share a Higher Education Example?

Imagine you teach an undergraduate literature course in which students read Ray Bradbury's *Dandelion Wine*. As they are preparing for writing essays about the themes within the book, you ask students to record their chapter notes in mind maps. Students can save these maps and send them in as assignments, or they can open their accounts to allow for collaboration with others. Figure 5.2 shows the beginning of one student's notes for the fourth chapter.

Where Can I Learn More?

To learn more about the use of graphic organizers in general, we recommend the following resource:

> McKnight, K. S. (2010). *The teacher's big book of graphic organizers: 100 reproducible organizers that help kids with reading, writing, and the content areas.* San Francisco: Jossey-Bass.

FIGURE 5.2. MIND MAP CREATED WITH MINDMEISTER

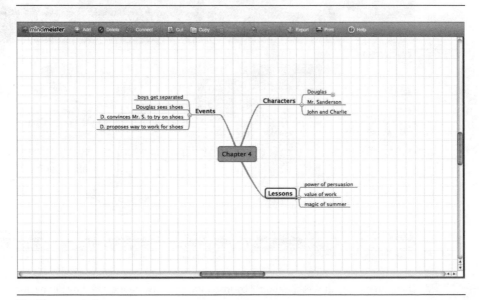

Used by permission.

Currently Available Tools

- Webspiration at www.mywebspiration.com/
- Mindmeister at www.mindmeister.com/

TABLE 5.1. DECISION-MAKING MATRIX—MIND-MAPPING OR GRAPHIC ORGANIZER TOOLS

	Webspiration	Mindmeister
Type of Tool	Organization	Organization
Problem It Solves	This tool helps instructors and students organize and represent information graphically. It works beyond text and focuses on relationships.	A common problem is getting students to organize ideas and see relationships. This tool helps instructors and students organize and represent information graphically. It works beyond text and focuses on relationships.
Cost	Free	Free
URL	www.mywebspiration.com/	www.mindmeister.com/
Description	This is a free Web-based tool. It allows users to create and share graphic organizers. They can also work collaboratively on the organizers in real time. The interface is very easy to understand.	This is a free Web-based tool. It allows users to create and share graphic organizers. They can also work collaboratively on the organizers in real time. The interface is very easy to understand.
Platform	Web	Web
Example (URL)	www.mywebspiration.com/ sites/default/files/filemanager/ image/AdvancedSiteMap_ Large.jpg	www.mindmeister.com/ 14250024/7-mind-mapping -examples-in-1-map
Best Used For	Creating a graphic organizer or visual image of a complex idea. The tool graphically shows relationships.	Creating a graphic organizer or visual image of a complex idea. The tool graphically shows relationships.
Level of Expertise	*Teacher:* Basic *Student:* Basic	*Teacher:* Basic *Student:* Basic
Cautions	Using graphic organizers can be simple or complex; make sure you understand when and how they are best used pedagogically.	Using graphic organizers can be simple or complex; make sure you understand when and how they are best used pedagogically.

(continued)

TABLE 5.1. (*continued*)

	Webspiration	Mindmeister
Overcoming Cautions	For the question of when and how to use graphic organizers, take the initiative and do advanced reading.	For the question of when and how to use graphic organizers, take the initiative and do advanced reading.
Accessibility Concerns	A general caution relates to the fact that this is a highly visual medium and is not accessible for learners who use screen readers. If you have students who use screen readers, this tool is not accessible. For students who require screen readers, design an alternative assignment or method of organizing.	A general caution relates to the fact that this is a highly visual medium and is not accessible for learners who use screen readers. If you have students who use screen readers, this tool is not accessible. For students who require screen readers, design an alternative assignment or method of organizing.
Special Equipment	None	None
Additional Vocabulary	None	None
Training and Resources	www.mywebspiration.com/gettingstarted	www.mindmeister.com/help/index

CHAPTER SIX

SOCIAL BOOKMARKING

C an you remember the URL for that great blog posting you read last Thursday? We didn't think so. Few of us retain that kind of data. When we mark a URL as a favorite or bookmark it on a computer, it is tied to that one specific machine. Unless you have an impeccable memory, you may not recall that URL when you go to another computer. Social bookmarking allows you to use a Web-based service to bookmark your favorite Web sites so that you can access them from any computer with Internet connectivity. No more remembering! Further, you tag these bookmarks using your own organizational code and can search through the bookmarks of like-minded readers. Bookmarks can be labeled as private or public and shared with colleagues, students, or even parents. This chapter introduces you to the idea of social bookmarking and describes how such tools can be used to organize both personal bookmarks and class resources.

What Is the Tool?

A social bookmarking tool is a Web-based means of storing and organizing URLs. For example, a user saves the URL information with a description of the resource and "tags" the content with her own organizational code. An article on the use of social bookmarking might be tagged as "social_bookmarking," "Web_2.0," "social_networking," "bookmarking," and more. Often the tool will recommend tags, and these tags are used for searching later. After a resource is saved within the tool, the user can access that resource from any computer with Internet connectivity. As long as the user remembers her log-in and password, her entire collection of links or resources is available.

Further, once the user saves a resource, she can see the popularity of the source by seeing who else has saved the same link. With this information, clever researchers can follow the bookmarks of like-minded users and possibly find additional resources they did not know of. It is a way of browsing through other users' publicly tagged resources, all organized by themes and tags.

Finally, users can share their resources with others by giving the URLs of their sites. For example, we could send you to a collection of URLs used for a presentation by giving you the unique URL for that whole collection. This is an economical way of organizing and sharing Web-based materials with specific audiences.

What Problem Does It Solve?

Social bookmarking solves several problems in regard to organization and portability of resources. On the personal front, the tool remembers for you and is not tied to any one computer. Therefore, you can move about freely and keep your bookmarks with you; as long as you have a computer with access to the Internet, you have your personal stash of information. Further, the nature of tagging helps organizationally challenged users keep content grouped together according to popular themes. For example, if you need to find a resource about civil disobedience that you saved, the tool lists your tags. Chances are good that you tagged the resource with a recognizable descriptor, like "civil_disobedience" or "activism" or "Thoreau." Seeing the tags directs you to the right place. What is more, social bookmarking solves the problem of having to constantly update Web pages if you want to share your links. By keeping the links within the tool and directing others to the unique URL that gives access to everything tagged under one descriptor, you do not have to update a page every time you add a new resource; the tool automatically updates the list.

Social bookmarking can also solve a problem related to research. As mentioned earlier, once a user saves a resource, it is possible to determine the popularity of the source and which other users have saved the same link.

By drilling down further and investigating the users and their bookmarks, you may find hidden gems of literature and research that you did not know about. In short, social bookmarking becomes a research tool for adding to your collection of sources and literature.

Finally, social bookmarking can serve as a repository for class resources, solving the problem of organizing contributions from different users. If the tool allows the administrator to establish groups, students can save links to materials within a group area. In many cases, these tools also invite comments about the sources, increasing the likelihood of dialogue and critical thinking.

Is This Something Instructors or Students Use?

Both instructors and students can use social bookmarking. After all, both groups are scholars and by nature will want to save and organize their resources. With some tools, instructors can start a group-based set of tags to which students can add their resources.

Is This Tool for the Novice, Intermediate, or Expert?

This is a tool a novice can use.

Is There Special Equipment or Software Needed?

You only need a computer with Internet connectivity and a Web browser.

What Are Some Cautions About This Tool?

Perhaps the main concern of those who use social bookmarking is that their habits and quirks will be public if they do not remember to set their resources as private. The other caution we offer is that it pays to follow the recommended tags. If you invent your own unique tagging taxonomy, it will not be as easy to follow other users and their tags; plus, you may forget what you were thinking of if you get too creative with your tagging.

How Accessible Is This Tool to All Users?

For the most part, social bookmarking tools are accessible to persons with disabilities. The content stored in the URLs may not be accessible, but the social bookmarking sites themselves are. The listings are in plain text, and navigation is typically well labeled. Screen readers work on these sites.

What Additional Vocabulary Do I Need to Know?

Folksonomy—a taxonomy built by common use of tags, or socially shared descriptors

Tagging—the act of assigning a unique identifying term to an item

Can You Share a K–12 Example?

Imagine you teach middle school social studies, and you are beginning a unit on the American Civil War. You are going to ask students each to write a report on one of the key battles. You will allow them to use Internet sources along with print media, but you would like to suggest quality sites to get them started. You could create a Web page and list some of the best online resources you have found, but each time you find another new resource you'll need to update that page. That will require you to be at a computer that has editing software and to have the original file and a means to put the edited file back on the server.

Rather than mess with the Web page, you create a list of Web-based resources within your social bookmarking tool and tag them accordingly. You provide the URL to students and parents, giving them an organized list of sites you find

FIGURE 6.1. CIVIL WAR BOOKMARKS SHARED WITH DELICIOUS

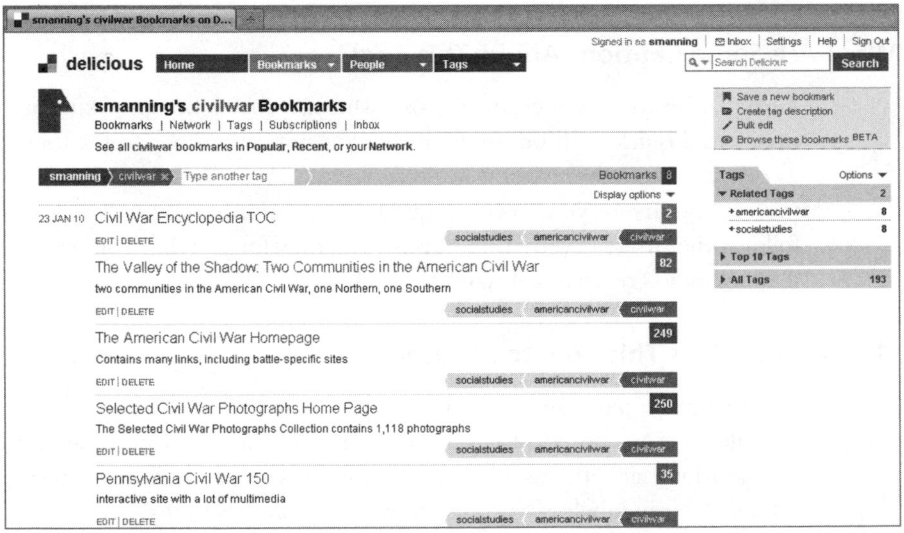

Used by permission.

appropriate. Figure 6.1 shows what that might look like from the student's or parent's viewpoint.

Can You Share a Higher Education Example?

Imagine you teach an online course about e-learning for educators. You want your students to find and share Web-based resources, and you want these resources to be available to them after the course ends. Further, because members will be able to see each other's profiles, you hope to build a network of alumni and students. You create a group on Diigo, a popular social bookmarking site, and teach students to save their resources to the group site. These resources are also saved within their personal archives. Members can see what the group has saved and resave those resources they personally find most helpful. Figure 6.2 shows what the student would see as they review the latest additions to the group area.

FIGURE 6.2. EDUCATIONAL GROUP IN DIIGO

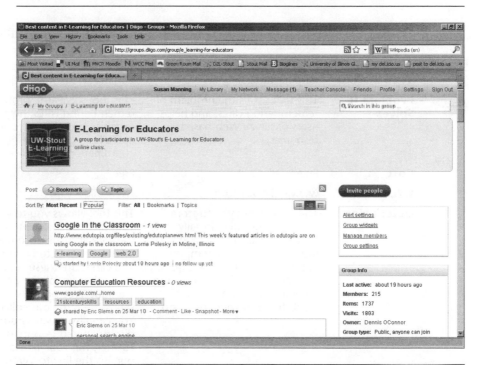

Used by permission.

Where Can I Learn More?

To learn more about social bookmarking, we recommend the following resources:

Hammond, T., Hannay, T., Lund, B., & Scott, J. (2005). Social bookmarking tools I. *D-Lib Magazine, 11*(4). Retrieved from http://dlib.org/dlib/april05/hammond/04hammond.html.

Lomas, C. P. (2005, May). 7 things you should know about social bookmarking. *Educause*. Retrieved from http://educause.edu/ir/library/pdf/ELI7001.pdf.

Currently Available Tools

- Delicious at www.delicious.com
- Diigo at www.diigo.com/

TABLE 6.1. DECISION-MAKING MATRIX—SOCIAL BOOKMARKING

	Delicious	Diigo
Type of Tool	Organization	Organization
Problem It Solves	This tool solves the problem of remembering URLs, and helps users organize Web-based resources.	This tool solves the problem of remembering URLs, helps users organize Web-based resources, and allows groups to coordinate research.
Cost	Free	Free
URL	www.delicious.com	www.diigo.com
Description	This tool allows you to store your favorite URLs virtually so they are accessible from any Internet-connected computer. You can share these resources with other people by providing a unique Web address that sends them to your collection.	This tool allows you to store your favorite URLs virtually so they are accessible from any Internet-connected computer. You can share these resources with other people by providing a unique Web address that sends them to your collection. You can also create groups and discuss shared resources. Further, this tool allows user to publish the link to Twitter simultaneously.

TABLE 6.1. (*continued*)

	Delicious	Diigo
Platform	Web	Web
Best Used For	Staying organized, sharing resources, and conducting personal research	Staying organized, sharing resources, and conducting personal research
Level of Expertise	*Teacher:* Basic *Student:* Basic	*Teacher:* Basic *Student:* Basic
Cautions	If you save bookmarks and do not label them as private, the whole world has access to your collection. Also, be careful not to get too creative with your tagging. If you do, others won't be able to search as easily because they may not appreciate your method of classifying and coding information.	If you save bookmarks and do not label them as private, the whole world has access to your collection. Also, be careful not to get too creative with your tagging. If you do, others won't be able to search as easily because they may not appreciate your method of classifying and coding information.
Overcoming Cautions	Make sure you make personal bookmarks private if you don't want others to see them, or create a second account. As for tagging, select from the suggested tags as these are the most readily searched tags for that idea.	Make sure you make personal bookmarks private if you don't want others to see them, or create a second account. As for tagging, select from the suggested tags as these are the most readily searched tags for that idea.
Accessibility Concerns	These tools are fairly accessible. They can be read with a screen reader and are easily navigable.	These tools are fairly accessible. They can be read with a screen reader and are easily navigable.
Special Equipment	None	None
Additional Vocabulary	*Tagging, folksonomy*	*Tagging, folksonomy*
Training and Resources	http://delicious.com/help	www.diigo.com/learn_more

CHAPTER SEVEN

VIRTUAL STORAGE AND FILE MANAGEMENT

Computer storage is like a high school letter jacket or a house; with time, it seems you outgrow it all too quickly. Think about a computer from seven years ago and compare how much data you could store in that machine versus a newer model. Such external devices as flash drives and portable hard drives have certainly made it easier to store and move files, but what if you need to get that huge file to a friend in another part of the world? That's where virtual storage and file management come into play. In this chapter we review why you would want to use a Web-based virtual storage system.

What Is the Tool?

Virtual storage tools allow you to upload files to a secure server that someone else hosts. You can store the files or share them with others. Because such tools are Web based, you upload and download through a browser.

What Problem Does It Solve?

If you need to send a colleague a 30 MB file, will your e-mail system allow it? Chances are you will not be able to send the file. With a virtual storage system, however, you could upload the file and make a link available to the colleague, who could then download from that link. That's the primary problem virtual storage solves. Secondarily, if you want to pay for a subscription to have more space, virtual storage also makes it possible to safely back up your hard drive.

Is This Something Instructors or Students Use?

This is a tool that both instructors and students can use. By nature of our collaborative work, we as instructors are more likely to swap big project files for research purposes than are students, but students can nevertheless use a service like this to send in assignments or access data they might need to complete work for their courses.

Is This Tool for the Novice, Intermediate, or Expert?

Because simple downloading is at work in most of these systems, a novice can use the tools. However, understanding what you're signing up for and what features are really necessary may push this into the realm of the intermediate-level user.

Is There Special Equipment or Software Needed?

The best tools only require an Internet connection and a Web browser.

What Are Some Cautions About This Tool?

In theory, if you do business with a reputable company that has a proven track record, your data will be safe and secure. That said, do your research and consider multiple backups if you think it is warranted (for example, save to an external drive as well as uploading the file). If the file you are working on relates to your dissertation and one-of-a kind research, you know how protective you'll get.

How Accessible Is This Tool to All Users?

For the most part, these tools are accessible. The file storage services have mainly drag-and-drop features, but there is often the option to work from a text-based menu.

What Additional Vocabulary Do I Need to Know?

You don't need any additional vocabulary.

Can You Share a K–12 Example?

Let's imagine you teach a high school biology course. You want your students to experience problem-based learning by addressing an environmental concern in your community. Tests conducted by state environmental agencies, archived video files, newscasts, interviews, and other documents are among the data you would like them to consider. You also want them to have access to these data after school hours, and to add to the collection. You upload what data you have into a storage service and make that available to students. At any time, in school or from home, students can access and add to the folder. Figure 7.1 shows what students might see as they access the folder from home. They can download a video, a PowerPoint file, and other images and documents to use in their work. Later, they can upload their own resources.

Can You Share a Higher Education Example?

You give your Psychology 101 students an opportunity to create a slide show in lieu of a formal paper. Some of the productions are too large to be e-mailed or uploaded within the course management system. Using a service that allows for the transfer of large amounts of data, the students upload their files. On the receiving end, you are notified via e-mail when a file is ready for you to download. You are given a specific URL to start the process. Figure 7.2 shows how easy it is to upload and send files using this process. Students can also use the same tool to send files to one another, which could be very helpful as they work on collaborative projects.

Where Can I Learn More?

If you choose to investigate virtual storage tools, start with a simple search using whatever search engine you prefer. As you find comparable materials, be sure you read carefully to make sure the tools have the features you need. Aside from whether the tool is free or requires a paid subscription, you'll want to look at whether users need an account to access your materials as well as whatever safeguards the company puts in place to secure your files.

FIGURE 7.1. VIRTUAL STORAGE CABINET FOR CLASS MATERIALS ON DRIVEHQ

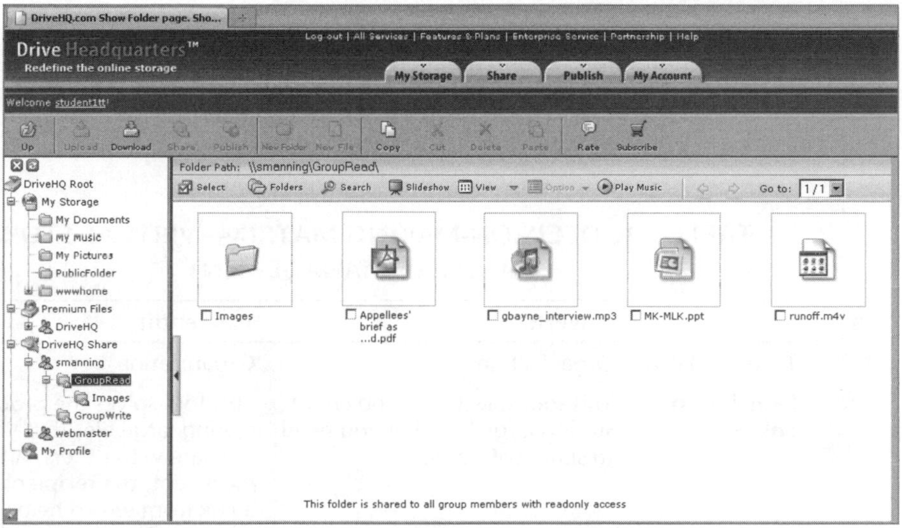

Used by permission.

FIGURE 7.2. YOUSENDIT UPLOAD FORM

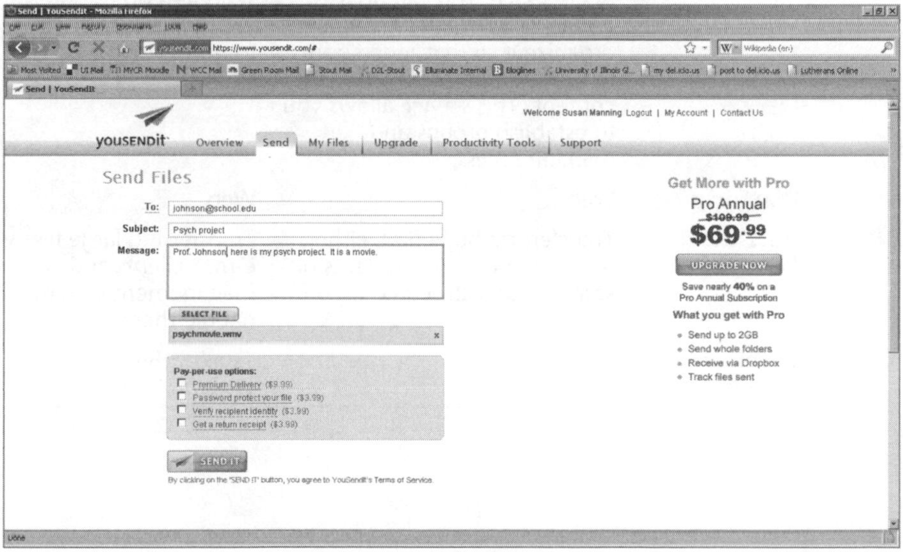

Used by permission.

Currently Available Tools

- DriveHQ at www.drivehq.com
- FileDen at www.fileden.com
- YouSendIt at www.yousendit.com

TABLE 7.1. DECISION-MAKING MATRIX—VIRTUAL STORAGE AND FILE MANAGEMENT

	DriveHQ	YouSendIt
Type of Tool	Organization	Organization
Problem It Solves	This tool solves the problem of storing large files that you need to share with others.	This tool solves the problem of storing large files that you need to share with others. After the file is sent, the recipient receives a link from which he or she can download within a week.
Cost	Free or inexpensive	Free or inexpensive
URL	www.drivehq.com	www.yousendit.com
Description	A free account allows for 1 GB of file space. You can upload and store any kind of file and organize it so that others can have access and download the content. This service allows you to establish groups and manage access.	A free account allows you to send files up to 100 MB, which are then available for download for one week.
Platform	Web	Web
Best Used For	Transferring huge files, either from instructors to students or students to instructors	Transferring large files whenever e-mail clients and course management systems cannot handle them
Level of Expertise	*Teacher:* Basic *Student:* Basic	*Teacher:* Basic *Student:* Basic

TABLE 7.1. (*continued*)

	DriveHQ	YouSendIt
Cautions	In the free version of this tool, you cannot delete top-level folders that you may not need (for example, MyMusic). This doesn't affect functionality, only the look of the product. It is a little tricky to get groups set up. You need to be careful that you have the file permissions set correctly so students can see what you want.	Downloads expire after a week.
Overcoming Cautions	Spend the time to test! If you are using this to share information with your students, create a dummy account and log in so you can see how it behaves. While you're there, take some screen shots to help your students visualize what they should do.	Because downloads expire after a week, be sure to independently alert the recipient that the file has been sent and give them the download link directly.
Accessibility Concerns	Because you can change the view from thumbnails to lists, an individual with a screen reader can access the information and navigate the site. It is a fairly accessible tool with no major limitations.	YouSendIt offers a variety of methods for using the service, providing multiple-browser support and desktop clients for multiple operating systems.
Special Equipment	None	None
Additional Vocabulary	None	None
Training and Resources	www.drivehq.com/help/helpframe.aspx	www.yousendit.com/support

PART THREE

TOOLS TO COMMUNICATE AND COLLABORATE

A famous soup manufacturer ran a series of television commercials in the Midwest showing consumers and cooks communicating using tin cans and strings. If you're over age forty, you might be able to visualize this and know where that idea comes from, but middle school–age children wouldn't understand. They don't play telephone with tin cans and strings like children of other eras did because they have cell phones! Nor does that age group handwrite letters to pen pals in other states or countries because they text their friends. Technology has completely transformed how and when we communicate. We are no longer limited by time or distance, thanks to mobile phones, discussion boards, instant messaging, and tweets.

Therefore, Part Three continues our discussion of Web-based tools by introducing the idea of using these tools to communicate and collaborate. Such tools can encourage instructor-to-instructor, instructor-to-student, student-to-student, and guest-to-class communication and collaboration efforts. In the online environment, these tools can be used to reduce transactional distance. Because online communication can give students the sense that their instructors or peers are available and accessible, students do not feel isolated and alone in the learning environment. There is a live person somewhere, always ready to communicate. And if the communication is not immediate, it often occurs within a matter of hours. For traditional courses or those that blend online and onground time, these tools can supplement in-class discussions. Finally, these tools allow instructors and students to collaborate at building a shared understanding and appreciation of the body of knowledge they're collectively shaping.

In this chapter we review tools used for voice and text discussion, Voice over Internet Protocol (VoIP), instant messaging and chat, blogs, wikis, microblogs, and Web conferencing.

CHAPTER EIGHT

DISCUSSION FORUMS

For instructors who teach online, whether completely online or using a blended (partially in-class and partially online) approach, they know the heart and soul of a course is its communication. Discussion forums are one tool instructors can use to encourage communication among students as they explore the course content and wrestle with pertinent questions. As an asynchronous tool, discussion forums allow those who engage in discussion to read and post any time; participation is not bound by real time. Further, discussion can occur using text or voice, depending on the capabilities of the tool.

Just in case the idea of discussion forums is foreign, think of a recent situation in which you needed technical assistance related to a product you purchased. Chances are good that you were directed to a company Web site and were instructed to peruse the frequently asked questions (FAQs). From there, you may have been encouraged to read through consumer posts of similar problems and their solutions. This is, in a manner of speaking, a consumer version of a discussion forum. The communication was problem centered and collaborative, and was not bound by time. These same conditions exist in the educational context.

Most instructors who use discussion forums do so to encourage student-to-student communication and collaboration. The pedagogy is much the same as it is in traditional, face-to-face education, with the aim of encouraging critical examination of the subject matter or promoting collaboration (Jonassen, Howland, Marra, & Crismond, 2008; Palloff & Pratt, 2003). A weekly discussion question about the course content might be at the center of a discussion, or a discussion forum may be a restricted area for group members to work on a collaborative project. It could even be a social area for students to swap homework tips or share clean jokes. What defines this form of communication as a discussion is the back-and-forth discourse, similar to discussion in real time. However, what sets online discussion apart from its classroom cousin is that in the online environment, every voice has the opportunity to be heard. Because the communication occurs asynchronously, even quieter or reticent students have the ability to post and be read with the same level of respect as their more aggressive peers. Asynchronous discussion levels the playing field. It simply doesn't matter who posts first. Furthermore, because the communication is prepared and delivered without the pressure of real time, the writing can be thoughtfully composed and edited so that it is deep and reflective (Palloff & Pratt, 2003).

What Is the Tool?

A discussion forum, whether text-based or voice-based, allows participants to post their ideas in writing or voice and to connect those ideas to others' comments and thoughts.

Course Management Systems

By far, the majority of discussion tools used in education are housed within course management systems, such as Blackboard or Moodle. These keep access to class discussions restricted through passwords. However, it is entirely possible to find stand-alone tools that support asynchronous discussion, either as free, open-source tools or as paid, licensed models. The degree of security and privacy is dependent on the tool and your administrative rights and abilities.

Text or Voice

The most common form of discussion occurs in a text-only format. By completing a Web-based form, each author creates a unique posting that is attached to the greater forum. These posts or messages are displayed in two ways. They may be listed as chronological, only showing the posts in time sequence. Or, they could be "threaded," connected in such a way as to graphically represent who responded to whom. A chronological example we will share in the chapter is Ning Groups.

Voice-based discussions operate in the same manner, but allow for respondents to record their voices and post the recordings in place of text. Depending on the software, the posts or messages can be displayed as chronological or threaded. This is a great tool for English as a Second Language and other language courses as a way of encouraging students to use vocabulary and practice with language conventions. It also humanizes the online environment for everyone when students and faculty can truly hear one another, complete with inflections and emotions.

What Problem Does It Solve?

Discussion forums solve several problems. The primary contribution is something we never have enough of—time. Instead of requiring students to be present at a specific time to give immediate responses, discussion forums promote asynchronous communication. Respondents thus have time to think and self-edit. In theory, discussion forums should solve the problem of having students "shoot from the hip" to give ill-formed, shallow responses. Also, because all students have sufficient time to form their responses, the "first posters" do not necessarily garner more attention. Someone who posts a day later may have a wonderful, rich idea that warrants just as much attention from the group. Finally, as participants comment on each other's ideas, synergy builds and new ideas flourish in the asynchronous environment.

Is This Something Instructors or Students Use?

Instructors have the administrative responsibility of creating the discussion forums and directing students to participate. Although students might do most of the posting, instructors must monitor and facilitate what happens in discussion. Meaningful discussions don't run themselves!

Is This Tool for the Novice, Intermediate, or Expert?

Fundamentally, getting a discussion forum up and running requires novice-level skills. However, it takes a master to facilitate really well!

Is There Special Equipment or Software Needed?

For text-based discussion, only a Web browser is needed. For voice communication, depending on the software, a microphone and headset might be required.

What Are Some Cautions About This Tool?

Cautions regarding discussion forums fall into two categories: pedagogy and security. The security concerns are only evident if you choose a tool that resides outside a course management system and doesn't have password protection for individual students. If a student posts publicly, it may be considered a violation of his or her privacy rights as a student. Therefore, make sure you either use a password-protected tool or have permission from each student.

In regard to pedagogy, you need to monitor discussion. Derogatory comments or inappropriate discourse would create an environment antithetical to what institutions of learning desire. Make sure you provide students with clear information about "netiquette" and your expectations. While you're at it, be sure to cover information about plagiarism so your students know you expect them to post original material or material that they have properly cited.

How Accessible Is This Tool to All Users?

Discussion tools get mixed reviews for accessibility depending on several factors. If a text-based tool is housed within a course management system that uses frames, navigation and use of such assistive technologies as screen readers may be awkward at best, impossible at worst. However, there may be other systems that are fully accessible for individuals with screen readers. Further, if a tool has audio with no text support, users with hearing impairments cannot participate. That said, most audio tools allow for posting text along with or in lieu of the audio. Because accessibility reviews are wholly dependent on the tool, research this area carefully before selecting a tool.

What Additional Vocabulary Do I Need to Know?

Asynchronous—not occurring in real time

Facilitation—the act of keeping the conversation going or probing for additional information, done by instructors

Open source—a type of software that is not purchased or licensed. You do not pay for the product; the code or software is freely available for you to install on your own server. You can customize the product however you wish, but this also means you have to support the product. In many cases this goes well beyond the average instructor's skills.

Netiquette—rules or protocol for keeping online communication respectful and civil

Threaded—used to describe one way of graphically displaying discussion posts that shows the relationship between comments

Can You Share a K–12 Example?

You teach eighth-grade language arts in a differentiated classroom that includes students from Laos. In small groups, all students are capable of sustaining conversations. You want your class to read the short story *Flowers for Algernon* by Daniel Keyes and create their own alternative endings, but you are concerned that the second language learners may not have the necessary writing skills. You establish an account with VoiceThread, a product that allows users to leave audio or text comments about an image or short video. Their assignment is to respond to a question posed by the instructor using voice or text and propose alternative endings. Students have their own identities within your account, represented by individual images. Figure 8.1 shows what students see when they come to the site. Students listen to your instructions and then record their own alternative endings. If they don't like the recordings, they can delete and start over. They

FIGURE 8.1. SAMPLE PAGE AT VOICETHREAD

Used by permission.

can also listen to the views of their fellow students. Each of the small icons or photos surrounding the image of the book cover is a separate voice comment from a peer. While two-thirds of your students work on a written assignment in the classroom, the other third accesses the site through the school's computer lab. Keep in mind that because this tool is asynchronous, students could do this assignment out of class, as well.

Can You Share a Higher Education Example?

Imagine you teach a course based on a book titled *The Technology Toolbelt for Teaching* (yes, imagine!). It could be offered as faculty development or pre-service education for aspiring K–12 teachers. You want to host a discussion about the use of discussion forums, but do not want this to be housed within a traditional course management system. Using a social networking tool, such as Ning, you

FIGURE 8.2. DISCUSSION FORUM CREATED IN NING

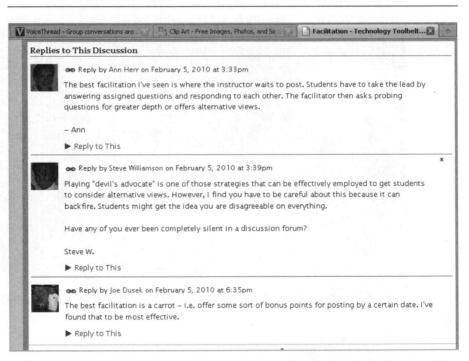

Used by permission.

establish a discussion area for this purpose. Students can join for free. Figure 8.2 shows what that interface might look like as students post text about the pedagogy of discussion forums.

Where Can I Learn More?

Numerous authors have written about the use of discussion forums as a pedagogical tool, because facilitation is a primary skill for the masterful online instructor. The following books are particularly helpful for understanding the role of the facilitator and the skills needed.

Collison, G., Elbaum, B., Haavind, S., & Tinker, A. (2000). *Facilitating online learning*. Madison, WI: Atwood.

Conrad, R., & Donaldson, J. (2004). *Engaging the online learner*. San Francisco: Jossey-Bass.

Palloff, R. M., & Pratt, K. (2007). *Building online learning communities: Effective strategies for the virtual classroom* (2nd ed.). San Francisco: Jossey-Bass.

Currently Available Tools

- Ning Social Network (and the discussion tool) at www.ning.com
- Yahoo! Groups at http://groups.yahoo.com
- Google Groups at http://groups.google.com
- VoiceThread at http://voicethread.com
- Wimba Voice at www.wimba.com/products/wimba_voice

TABLE 8.1. DECISION-MAKING MATRIX—DISCUSSION FORUMS

	VoiceThread	Ning Social Network and the Discussion Tool
Type of Tool	Communication and collaboration	Communication and collaboration
Problem It Solves	This product solves the problem of allowing people to communicate in a discussion forum, without a formal course management system. Specifically, it allows people to record and post their ideas orally and asynchronously. It offers an alternative to writing posts, although users can also leave written comments.	This product solves the problem of allowing people to communicate in a discussion forum, without a formal course management system. It allows people to write and post thoughts on topics or issues asynchronously. There is no need for real-time communication.
Cost	Free or inexpensive	Free or inexpensive
URL	www.voicethread.com	www.ning.com
Description	VoiceThread is a social tool that allows users to upload images (slides), and then post their ideas through voice. It lets listeners or viewers leave additional comments through voice. The product allows for recording via a microphone or telephone. Individual "threads" can be made private or public.	Ning is a social networking tool that allows users to create pages and spaces for other users to join. Within a network, the creator can establish discussion forums to host asynchronous conversations. Users can control whether they view these discussions as threaded or chronological.
Platform	Web	Web
Example (URL)	http://voicethread.com/ #q.b409.i848804	http://techtools.ning.com/
Best Used For	Having students generate oral responses to a question, topic, or piece of work. Students can also practice listening skills.	Hosting asynchronous discussions when users do not have access to a similar tool within a course management system. This tool is also good for when you want discussions to include voices outside the academic community (guests, industry experts, alumni).
Level of Expertise	*Teacher:* Basic *Student:* Basic	*Teacher:* Basic *Student:* Basic

TABLE 8.1. (*continued*)

	VoiceThread	Ning Social Network and the Discussion Tool
Cautions	Privacy is always a concern. Also, be prepared to offer a little additional technical support because this involves audio.	Privacy is the main caution. In addition, an unmonitored discussion may lead to postings that are inappropriate for academic discourse.
Overcoming Cautions	Make sure you know how to set privacy controls. One user can have multiple identities, so a teacher could establish identities for each student under his account, bypassing privacy concerns. Also, prepare some introductory information, or link students to help sheets for microphone and other audio trouble.	Users must create accounts and ask permission to join your network. Instruct students on how to protect their privacy. As a network administrator, carefully control who is able to join the network, and monitor postings.
Accessibility Concerns	There are several accessibility issues with this tool. It cannot be accessed with a keyboard because of the Flash components. Text alternatives are not possible. So although the site offers audio, users with screen readers cannot navigate the site.	This product is not very friendly to blind users who require screen readers, in that it is difficult for them to navigate to create accounts. However, it is possible to use JavaScript to get around that, if you know someone who can code for you. The JavaScript can allow users to sign in without the use of a pointer device like a mouse. Frankly, this is beyond the average instructor's level of expertise.
Special Equipment	Speakers and microphones (only needed for recording)	None
Additional Vocabulary	*Asynchronous*	*Asynchronous*
Training and Resources	http://voicethread.com/support/faq/	http://creators.ning.com/

CHAPTER NINE

VOICE OVER INTERNET PROTOCOL

Did you use a telephone today? If so, you understand the value of immediate voice communication. That same kind of communication is available in Voice over Internet Protocol (VoIP) and provides another way for instructors to reach out to students. VoIP tools allow users to communicate from a distance in real time (synchronously) using their voices, much like the telephone. VoIP technology can be used for class discussions, small-group meetings, or one-on-one meetings with students. You can also use it to bring guest lecturers into your classroom. This chapter explores the uses for VoIP tools in the academic environment.

What Is the Tool?

VoIP is a communication tool that converts sound from analog to digital and sends it over Internet networks. Using VoIP is similar to using a telephone, but it involves the Internet. The caller initiates the call from a computer and speaks into his microphone. The receiver hears the call through her computer speakers and speaks back using her microphone. Communication is immediate.

In some cases, these tools also allow video conferencing so the parties can see webcam streams of each other. The tool may also support text chat and file sharing so that users can communicate additional information during a call.

What Problem Does It Solve?

The value of the human voice cannot be underestimated in terms of its ability to convey warmth as well as conviction through such nonverbal elements as tone and inflection. Especially for those teaching at a distance, these components may be missing in text-only communication. As Betts (2008) argues, adding personalized communication through voice may increase student engagement in distance education. Research by Day, Wood, Scutter, and Astachnowicz (2003) likewise supports the idea that synchronous voice communication can relieve transactional distance between students and instructors, thereby helping to build community and enhancing engagement.

Because using VoIP is similar to using the telephone, let's consider where VoIP solves additional problems beyond those solved by the telephone. Some VoIP is free; you don't have to use a paid service to communicate. Further, VoIP supports free conferencing: students can self-organize and hold small-group meetings free of charge and without the instructor.

Is This Something Instructors or Students Use?

Both instructors and students can use VoIP.

Is This Tool for the Novice, Intermediate, or Expert?

This is a tool a novice can use.

Is There Special Equipment or Software Needed?

To use a voice tool, you need a microphone and speakers. All computers come with the ability to handle sound these days, so no additional hardware or setup is required, but you do need to know how to turn up the volume or make sure your sound is not muted.

What Are Some Cautions About This Tool?

To use a Web-based VoIP tool, users must create accounts with the product. Any time you ask students to do this, you expose them to security and privacy concerns. If you teach young children, VoIP may not be an option for you unless you are the account holder and are supervising the use. However, if you work with adults, you can provide them with the choice of whether or not to participate. Tools come with preferences. You can instruct your students to set their privacy features so that they have maximum control over who sees them online. Strangers must ask permission to communicate and can be blocked if they become a nuisance.

Half-truths have circulated concerning computer viruses and worms spread through VoIP products. Basic voice communication does not leave one's computer vulnerable to these kinds of threats. However, file transfer features could make it possible to transmit viruses and worms, and students should be forewarned.

How Accessible Is This Tool to All Users?

As you might expect, VoIP is much more accessible to persons with visual impairments than to those with hearing impairments. Blind users who require screen readers report successful navigation and use. Users who are hearing impaired would probably not select this product unless it had adequate text options or could allow for Web conferencing that displays a sign language interpreter or has closed captioning. Therefore, consider your audience when implementing this type of tool.

What Additional Vocabulary Do I Need to Know?

Synchronous—occurring in real time

Webcam—a camera device that allows video to be broadcast over the Internet

Can You Share a K–12 Example?

You are teaching third grade, and you begin a unit on Native Americans. Your textbook introduces students to the Chippewa, but you live in a region where there are no Chippewa residents. Using Skype, you arrange for your class to interview a Chippewa person thousands of miles away. The class can ask him questions, and he can answer immediately. He installs a webcam, allowing the class to see him so he can share artifacts on the screen. Because the Skype interface allows for desktop sharing, where one user sees what is displayed on another user's computer screen, the guest could share photos that way, too. Figure 9.1 shows the interface and what students would see if you were to project the screen.

Can You Share a Higher Education Example?

You teach an online business course at a community college. You ask your students to plan a presentation together, and you put them in groups of five. Although you provide an asynchronous discussion forum for them to use for

FIGURE 9.1. SKYPE VIDEO CALL

Used by permission.

planning purposes, several students decide to talk about their presentation in a conference call on Tinychat. Figure 9.2 shows what that interface might look like, and includes the text chat going on simultaneously.

Where Can I Learn More?

To learn more about VoIP, We recommend the following resource:

> Fryer, W. (2005). Skype in the classroom. *Tools for the Teks: Integrating Technology in the Classroom.* Retrieved from www.wtvi.com/teks/ 05_06_articles/skype-in-the-classroom.html.

Currently Available Tools

- Skype at www.skype.com
- Google Talk at either www.google.com/talk/ (for talk only) or www.google .com/chat/video (to add video to your talk)
- Tinychat at www.tinychat.com

FIGURE 9.2. GROUP VIDEO CONFERENCE USING TINYCHAT

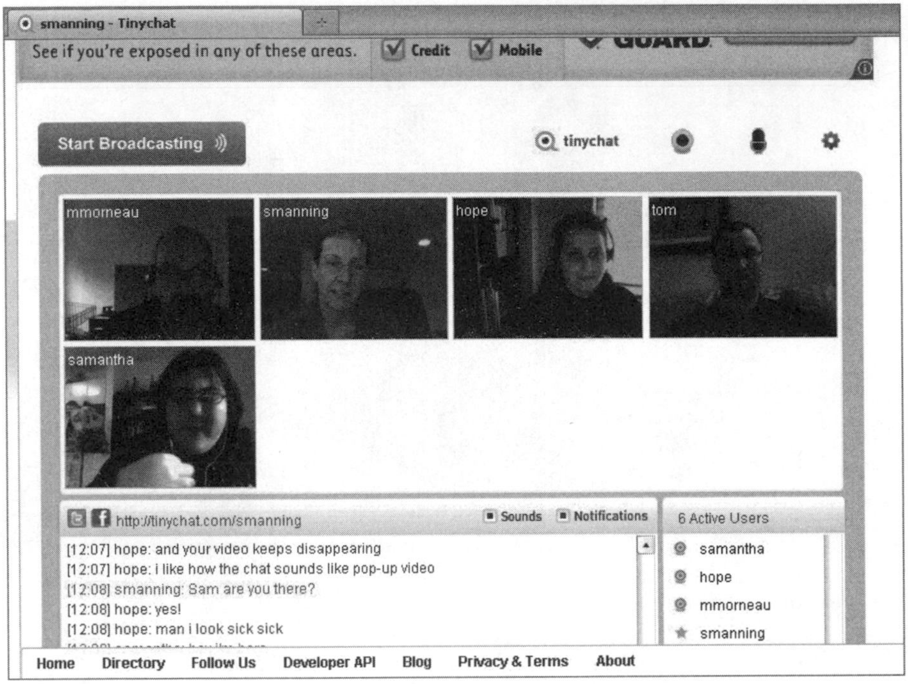

Used by permission.

TABLE 9.1. DECISION-MAKING MATRIX—VOICE OVER INTERNET PROTOCOL

	Skype	Tinychat
Type of Tool	Communication and collaboration	Communication and collaboration
Problem It Solves	This tool allows for immediate voice communication. It breaks down barriers of transactional distance. It doesn't have the cost of a cell phone, and it allows users to communicate globally.	This tool allows for immediate voice and video communication. It breaks down barriers of transactional distance.
Cost	Free or inexpensive	Free
URL	www.skype.com	www.tinychat.com

TABLE 9.1. (*continued*)

	Skype	Tinychat
Description	Skype is a VoIP tool that allows for voice chat, text chat, and video conferencing. You can exchange files and show other users your desktop. For a small charge, you can also call regular telephones from your computer and allow others to leave you voice mail.	This VoIP tool allows for video and voice chat for up to ten simultaneous webcam users. It also supports text chat and desktop sharing, and provides users with a whiteboard. A whiteboard is a shared space people can type or draw on.
Platform	Web	Web
Example (URL)	www.skype.com	http://tinychat.com/channel
Best Used For	Synchronous voice communication. This should probably be used in higher education, unless the teacher closely controls use among K–12 students.	Synchronous voice and video communication. Tinychat is definitely something for adult learners and not for unsupervised children.
Level of Expertise	*Teacher:* Basic *Student:* Basic	*Teacher:* Basic *Student:* Basic
Cautions	Using this tool may result in a loss of privacy. Although you control who is in your contacts list (and therefore who knows you are online and can contact you), you may occasionally receive a spam message.	Using this tool may result in a loss of privacy. Almost anyone can find your "room" and come in to chat.
Overcoming Cautions	Instruct students to set preferences so their identities are private. They can control who sees them online and who can contact them.	One user originates the chat. The others who join need to know that strangers could drop in, and users should discuss how the group would handle that.
Accessibility Concerns	This product is not accessible for hearing-impaired students, unless they have video conferencing abilities and you provide an interpreter or closed captioner.	Likewise, this product is not accessible for hearing-impaired students, unless they have video conferencing abilities and you provide an interpreter or closed captioner.
Special Equipment	Webcam (only for video), microphone, and speakers	Webcam (only for video), microphone, and speakers
Additional Vocabulary	*Synchronous Webcam*	*Synchronous Webcam*
Training and Resources	www.skype.com/getconnected	http://tinychat.com/about.html

CHAPTER TEN

INSTANT MESSAGING AND CHAT

Susan sits in her office grading papers. Meanwhile, in another state, a student in Susan's online class has a question about this week's assignment. Seeing that Susan's icon in Google Chat is active, the student types her question in the chat box and pushes the send button. Within three or four chat exchanges, the student has her answer, and Susan goes back to grading papers. This is the beauty of instant messaging or chat—immediate answers in short bursts of text conversation.

This chapter explores the convenience of chat: real-time, text-based communication. Chat is often included as a feature of course management systems and is available in stand-alone products, such as Google Chat or Yahoo! Messenger.

What Is the Tool?

Chat or instant messaging is a text-based, synchronous form of communication. Individuals type short notes back and forth to one another in real time. It can be part of a course management system or a stand-alone product that users install on their computers. Usually, in order to chat with someone, the user needs to know the other person's screen name, and has to add that individual to his or her list of contacts. Some chat products also allow for file transfers. Many of today's instant messaging products have added voice chat and mobile phone applications so that the products are portable.

What Problem Does It Solve?

Chat helps users solve immediate problems, because the communication is synchronous. It is most appropriate for quick questions that do not require lengthy explanations. In the same way that other synchronous tools allow students to feel better connected in the virtual classroom, the immediacy of chat can reduce transactional distance. Simply put, learners feel connected.

Before Web conferencing and voice tools became available to the masses, chat was used for group meetings in many online courses. The instructor announced a meeting time and place, students logged in, and the teacher facilitated the discussion. This method of group facilitation required a unique set of skills, including forethought in regard to structuring the time, an understanding of specific protocols for answering, fast typing abilities, and patience toward those who responded slowly. Frankly, many chat sessions embodied some level of chaos. Today, students may meet in chat rooms as they organize their collaborative projects, but the tools are most commonly used for one-on-one communication.

Is This Something Instructors or Students Use?

Both instructors and students use chat. They may chat with one another, or students may chat among themselves outside of class time.

Is This Tool for the Novice, Intermediate, or Expert?

This is a tool a novice can use.

Is There Special Equipment or Software Needed?

No special equipment is needed, but you do need to have the chat software installed on a computer with an Internet connection. There is a simple download process.

What Are Some Cautions About This Tool?

Loss of privacy is the foremost concern. If you make yourself available to your students through a service, and they know you are online, the rest of the world knows, too. If you leave your chat program running 24/7 (as many of us do), your students might believe you are available for work-related questions 24/7. Further, chat used to have a seedy history of hosting gatherings of unseemly types, so if you work with groups of students in chat, be sure the room is private and that strangers cannot wander into your conversation.

How Accessible Is This Tool to All Users?

Most of today's chat and instant messaging tools earn mixed reviews in terms of accessibility. Some of this depends on whether they have to be accessed exclusively with a keyboard. Users of such assistive technologies as screen readers need to learn how to manage settings so they can participate, so be aware that if you choose to use this tool in your instruction you may need to research those alternatives. Text-based chat or instant messaging does not exclude those with hearing impairments.

What Additional Vocabulary Do I Need to Know?

IM—the abbreviation for instant messaging or instant message

Synchronous—occurring in real time

Can You Share a K–12 Example?

Mindy, an online student in sixth grade, is working on a book report. She forgets what one concept means, but sees that her teacher is available in Google Chat.

FIGURE 10.1. SAMPLE INSTANT MESSAGING BETWEEN TEACHER AND STUDENT IN GOOGLE CHAT

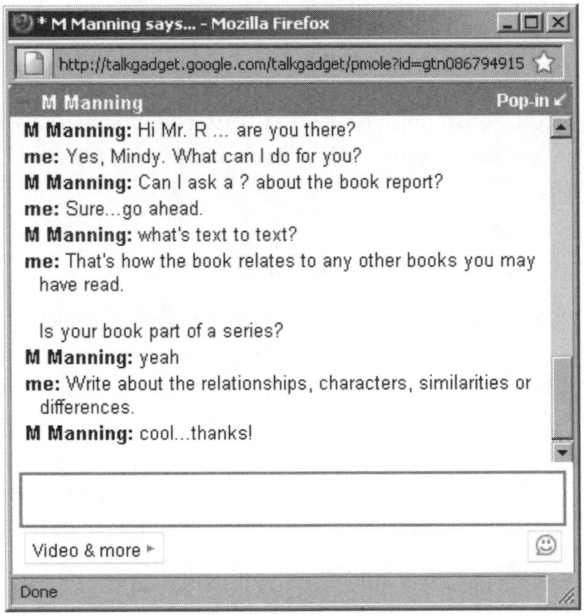

She sends a quick question, which is answered immediately. Mindy continues her work. Figure 10.1 depicts this brief conversation.

Can You Share a Higher Education Example?

Classmates Jill and George are in the same accounting class. Both are working on a spreadsheet assignment at home and see that the other is online. George asks Jill if she knows the correct formula for one of the columns. Jill coaches him through the task in a series of quick exchanges in Yahoo! Messenger. Figure 10.2 shows what that exchange might look like.

FIGURE 10.2. CONVERSATION BETWEEN CLASSMATES IN YAHOO! MESSENGER

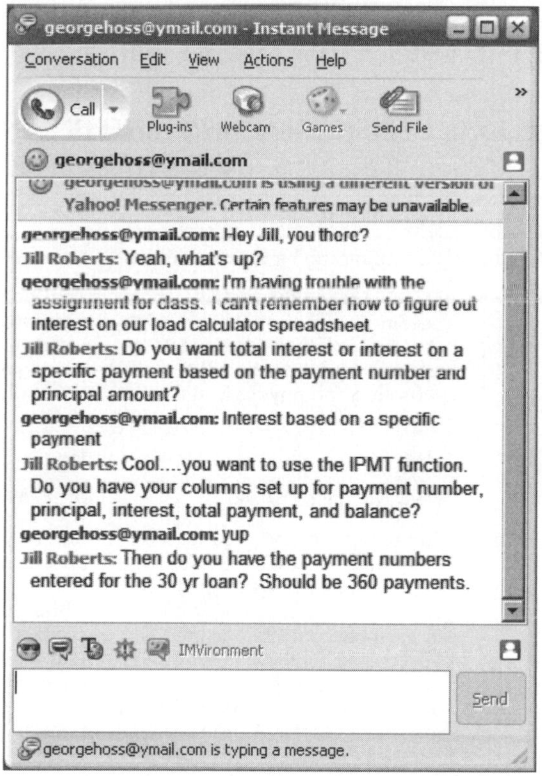

Where Can I Learn More?

To learn more about instant messaging and chat, we recommend the following resources:

Moore, G. S., Winograd, K., & Lange, D. (2001). *You can teach online.* Boston: McGraw-Hill.

Reynard, R. (2007, October 31). Tips for using chat as an instructional tool. *Campus Technology.* Retrieved from http://campustechnology.com/articles/2007/10/tips-for-using-chat-as-an-instructional-tool.aspx.

Currently Available Tools

- Google Chat at www.google.com/talk/
- Yahoo! Messenger at http://webmessenger.yahoo.com/
- AOL Instant Messenger at www.aim.com/

TABLE 10.1. DECISION-MAKING MATRIX—INSTANT MESSAGING AND CHAT

	Google Chat	Yahoo! Messenger
Type of Tool	Communication and collaboration	Communication and collaboration
Problem It Solves	This tool solves the problem of needing a quick answer and being at a distance. It allows students to ask quick questions in real time without being physically in the same location.	This tool solves the problem of needing a quick answer and being at a distance. It allows students to ask quick questions in real time without being physically in the same location.
Cost	Free	Free
URL	www.google.com/talk/	http://webmessenger.yahoo.com/
Description	Running in the background, this application sits on the user's desktop until he or she needs to communicate. Choosing from a list of personal contacts, the user selects a contact and sends a short message. The receiver must be online at the time to receive the message instantly. A short, back-and-forth text conversation begins.	Running in the background, this application sits on the user's desktop until he or she needs to communicate. Choosing from a list of personal contacts, the user selects a contact and sends a short message. The receiver must be online at the time to receive the message instantly. A short, back-and-forth text conversation begins.

TABLE 10.1. (*continued*)

	Google Chat	Yahoo! Messenger
Platform	Web	Web
Best Used For	Quick conversations and questions in real time	Quick conversations and questions in real time
Level of Expertise	*Teacher:* Basic *Student:* Basic	*Teacher:* Basic *Student:* Basic
Cautions	Once people know your username, they know it forever (or until you change it). That can result in a loss of privacy. Also, if you have the tool turned on 24/7, individuals might think It Is permissible to contact you 24/7.	Once people know your username, they know it forever (or until you change it). That can result in a loss of privacy. Also, if you have the tool turned on 24/7, individuals might think it is permissible to contact you 24/7.
Overcoming Cautions	Be judicious with turning it on and off. Create one account solely for instructional purposes and only use it when you consider yourself working.	Be judicious with turning it on and off. Create one account solely for instructional purposes and only use it when you consider yourself working.
Accessibility Concerns	Google Chat is not ideal for persons who use screen readers. Signing on is problematic and requires keyboarding.	Yahoo! Messenger is not ideal for persons who use screen readers. Signing on is problematic and requires keyboarding.
Special Equipment	No special equipment is needed if you are only text chatting. You do, however, need to install the chat software from Google.	No special equipment is needed if you are only text chatting. You do, however, need to install the chat software from Yahoo.
Additional Vocabulary	IM Synchronous	IM Synchronous
Training and Resources	www.google.com/support/talk/?hl=en	http://help.yahoo.com/l/us/yahoo/messenger/web/web1/

CHAPTER ELEVEN

BLOGS

Turn to any major media or news source, and you'll find a blog, a Web page that allows the reader to absorb the information and then comment. When the reader does this, the page becomes interactive and not static. Television broadcasters, celebrities, and respected publishers have blogs. Blogs are one of the earliest components of Web 2.0 that caught fire with the mainstream public. Even if you weren't publishing your own blog, chances are good that between 2002 and 2004 you read commentary from a blog on current issues, such as the Iraq War and Dan Rather's news reporting. The "blogosphere" began to shape what we read; but more important, it allowed average readers to comment and develop the story further. In an educational context, blogs have served as information sources and publishing venues for instructors and students. This chapter explores blogs as an instructional tool.

What Is the Tool?

A blog is a type of Web page that allows readers to add comments. Also called Weblogs, many blogs imitate online diaries or journals; the author records events and insights on a regular basis. Others forms of blogs aggregate stories or news from multiple sources and republish links. For example, in education, Ray Schroeder's blog Online Learning Update searches for and digests news related to online learning and research (http://people.uis.edu/rschr1/onlinelearning/blogger.html).

One of the defining characteristics of a blog is that it is syndicated, meaning that users can subscribe to it using a Really Simple Syndication (RSS) feed so that they are alerted each time the blog is updated. Blogs are created and published using special software to allow for subscription and tracking. Some programs are more sophisticated than others, but most are Web based and free. The program vendor hosts the blog and provides the RSS feed. Examples of blogging Web sites are WordPress and Edublogs.

What Problem Does It Solve?

Blogs can solve several instructional problems, depending on how they are used. First, a blog can be used as a centralized communication vehicle when an instructor needs to share information across several courses. An instructor can publish news and announcements to a wider audience, or to parents of students, for example. A second problem blogs solve has to do with finding an authentic audience to read and provide feedback on student work. A blog can serve as a publishing medium for student work so that it is shared with a worldwide audience. Student authors then receive feedback and reactions that are authentic and diverse. When students are asked to journal in blogs, the practice and discipline of writing can only serve to strengthen their skills (Downes, 2009a; Duffy & Bruns, 2006). Finally and most simply, blogs can serve as sources of information when instructors ask students to research and follow specific blogs to review current events and insights.

Is This Something Instructors or Students Use?

Because blogs can be viewed as information sources and as venues for publishing, both instructors and students can use them. Either party can create or read blogs. Although research from the Pew Internet & American Life Project (Lenhart, Purcell, Smith, & Zickuhr, 2010) indicates that teen blogging has decreased from 28 percent to 14 percent of teens between 2006 and 2009, it is still reasonable to assume that teens know what blogs are and would have little difficulty starting blogs if they wanted to.

Is This Tool for the Novice, Intermediate, or Expert?

Reading a blog requires no real skills and is for the novice. However, publishing a blog may require an understanding of blogging technology approaching that of an intermediate user. Although most of the publishing software is straightforward (What You See Is What You Get [WYSIWYG]), you may need to dig deeper into the interface to make the blog do what you want (for example, to learn how to moderate comments). Then again, products are becoming more user-friendly every month. One service, Posterous, advertises that you can e-mail them the content and they will create the blog for you. Others allow for automatic photo resizing if you want to add images. You'll only learn about these features as you investigate individual products.

Is There Special Equipment or Software Needed?

No special equipment is needed, but you do need to access the Web-based site provided by the vendor because it contains the programming code that allows you to write and publish a blog with an RSS feed. There are an abundance of free Web-based tools available for this. You can find blogging products by running a simple search, examples of which include WordPress, Blogger, and Posterous.

What Are Some Cautions About This Tool?

The primary concerns for this tool are loss of privacy and receiving questionable comments or SPAM. When you create an account with a blog service, you must register an e-mail address. You can determine whether your blog will be included in search results, but fundamentally this means you have an open page on the Internet. If you want a worldwide audience, you'll get a worldwide audience! That also means your blog is a target for SPAM and offensive comments. Turning on the feature to moderate these comments usually addresses the problem. For younger students, there are services that protect their identities and allow the teacher to control who can see their blogs.

The issue of anonymity is a blessing and a curse when using blogs for instructional purposes. If you want students to answer a controversial question honestly and therefore allow anonymous posts, you have no way of awarding points if the students' responses are intended as part of a graded assignment.

How Accessible Is This Tool to All Users?

For the most part, blogs are accessible to persons with various disabilities. As a straightforward text medium, most blogging tools are easy for students with screen readers to navigate. Although a pointing device may be needed for toolbars on the blog's administrative interface, entry of text and reading of text are accessible.

What Additional Vocabulary Do I Need to Know?

Blogroll—usually a sidebar on a blog in which the author shares favorite blogs and links. Following these can result in finding new resources.

Moderated comments—statements from blog readers that do not become visible until the blog administrator moderates and gives permission.

Really Simple Syndication (RSS)—technology that allows others to subscribe to your blog so that whenever you make an entry, they are informed.

WYSIWYG—What You See Is What You Get, meaning that as you enter and change text, it appears as it would when published. You do not need to know computer coding to get text to be bold or italicized, for example.

Can You Share a K–12 Example?

To encourage students' reading, writing, and analysis, you subscribe to a type of aggregated blog service, TweenTribune. Published since 2009, this service selects news stories of interest to children ages eight through fourteen and aggregates the links for subscribers. The stories are framed as essential questions to entice readers to comment, a fundamental shift in thinking about how to read (and publish) news. An example of an essential question would be "What technology could you absolutely not live without?" As a teacher, you create a free account and select the stories you want your students to read. You can tailor these according to your curriculum. Students establish accounts through your administration (and careful guidance), and they can read and respond to the stories you choose to display. Figure 11.1 shows a student's comments in response to a story about teens' use of technology. What is particularly noteworthy about this service is that teachers must supervise the setup of student accounts and moderate comments. This affords a higher level of personal security for the students. In addition, the students cannot add one- or two-word comments; the posts must be at least twenty-five words in length, or they will not be accepted.

Can You Share a Higher Education Example?

A group of scientists at the Bradley Laboratory of Drexel University have taken to blogging as a way to promote their research. Called Useful Chemistry, this blog can be followed by students in chemistry classes around the world. Reading the blog becomes the jumping-off point for discussions, whether in traditional or online courses. Further, students following the blog benefit from perspectives other than those of their own professors. Students can also interact with the researchers, and comment or ask questions independent of class work. Figure 11.2 shows a sample of this blog.

FIGURE 11.1. SAMPLE BLOG POST WRITTEN BY A YOUNG STUDENT IN TWEENTRIBUNE

Used by permission.

Where Can I Learn More?

There are several books you might want to consult related to the use of blogs in education. Two such books are

Richardson, W. (2008). *Blogs, wikis, podcasts, and other powerful Web tools for classrooms*. Thousand Oaks, CA: Corwin Press.

Rosenberg, S. (2009). *Say everything: How blogging began, what it's becoming, and why it matters*. New York: Crown.

FIGURE 11.2. BLOG MAINTAINED BY HIGHER EDUCATION FACULTY AT DREXEL UNIVERSITY

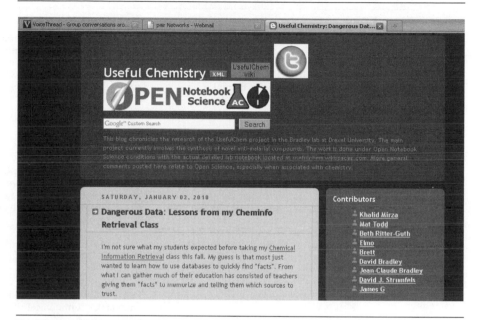

Used by permission.

Currently Available Tools

- TweenTribune at http://www.tweentribune.com
- WordPress at http://wordpress.com/
- Blogger at www.blogger.com/start
- Edublogs at http://edublogs.org/
- Posterous at http://posterous.com/

TABLE 11.1. DECISION-MAKING MATRIX—BLOGS

	TweenTribune	WordPress
Type of Tool	Communication and collaboration	Communication and collaboration
Problem It Solves	Getting students to know how to read news and then apply critical thinking to what they read can be problematic. This tool gets kids to read and digest current events. It prompts them to write about what they've read.	It can be a problem to find authentic audiences to read and comment on student work. When this tool is used to support writing, students have an authentic, worldwide audience and receive valuable feedback on writing.
Cost	Free	Free
URL	http://tweentribune.com/	http://wordpress.com/
Description	Teachers subscribe to this service, which aggregates news of interest for young readers. By establishing class accounts, teachers can then assign specific stories for students to read and respond to. Students practice critical thinking and writing.	This tool allows the teacher to create a blog to publish student work. The teacher might also use the same tool to publish her own work, shared across several courses.
Platform	Web	Web
Best Used For	Critical thinking and publishing writing	Publishing writing (instructor or student) or communicating with a class
Level of Expertise	*Teacher:* Basic *Student:* Basic	*Teacher:* Basic *Student:* Basic
Cautions	There are very few cautions, because this site follows COPPA guidelines.	If using this tool with children under the age of thirteen, be sure to protect their privacy and refer to the Children's Online Privacy Protection Act (COPPA) guidelines.
Overcoming Cautions	Teachers control what is published, including usernames.	If students are making blog entries, have them only use first names so as to maintain privacy. Further, do not allow students to post photos or give out other identifying information.
Accessibility Concerns	There are no obvious concerns—the tool passes most accessibility tests.	This tool passes most accessibility tests. Students with screen readers can navigate the software and published blogs.
Special Equipment	None	None
Additional Vocabulary	*Moderated comments*	*Blogroll, moderated comments, RSS, WYSIWYG*
Training and Resources	http://tweentribune.com/content/tweentribune-classroom	http://en.support.wordpress.com/

CHAPTER TWELVE

WIKIS

Aside from being fun to say, wikis are an innovative, practical answer to collaborative writing. A wiki page allows a group of users to update and edit text collaboratively. Most wikis also support the inclusion of tables, charts, and images. This chapter reviews how wikis can be used for collaborative work among students and professionals, and for quick publishing of content.

What Is the Tool?

A wiki is a Web page that can be shared by a group and edited by anyone who has permission. In many cases, it is possible to subscribe to a wiki so that you are informed of changes and updates.

What Problem Does It Solve?

Ever try to write in a group? The document gets passed back and forth so many times, no one knows who contributed what. If collaboration relies solely on e-mail, one person's changes may not be noticed or included before another overwrites the idea. With a wiki, the history of the document is maintained, and all members see the latest version. Fundamentally, a wiki addresses the instructional problem of collaborative writing, allowing for a one-stop place for group authors to contribute to, edit, and even discuss the growing document.

Is This Something Instructors or Students Use?

Similar to a blog, a wiki could be viewed as an information source and as a venue for publishing. Both instructors and students can use wikis. In most cases, instructors establish wikis to which students then contribute collaboratively. However, instructors may also choose to create wikis for their own personal work, such as for sharing research with colleagues at different institutions.

Is This Tool for the Novice, Intermediate, or Expert?

Creating and maintaining a wiki are tasks that most novices can handle.

Is There Special Equipment or Software Needed?

No special equipment is needed, but you do need to subscribe to a service to create and host your wiki. There are an abundance of free, Web-based products available for this, such as PBWorks and Wikispaces. For a comparison of wikis, consider visiting www.wikimatrix.org.

What Are Some Cautions About This Tool?

The primary concern with this tool is loss of privacy. Similar to blogs, wikis make your work and your students' work publicly viewable. The good news is that because a wiki can be tightly controlled in terms of who can edit and contribute, it is not as likely that you'll receive questionable comments or SPAM.

Another caution is that students have to be trained on how to use a wiki or they may inadvertently erase someone else's work. Fortunately, there is a feature on almost every wiki to undo the damage, called a rollback, but an ounce of prevention is advised. Furthermore, some wikis do not support simultaneous editing. For example, if one student is making changes at the exact same time as another, she may accidentally cancel the changes another is making. Google Docs is a product that behaves like a wiki and allows for synchronous, simultaneous editing. Google Docs goes beyond being a wiki in that you can also create spreadsheets, presentations, and forms, not just traditional text documents. Furthermore, you can download the finished product from Google Docs into a variety of forms such as a Word file, PDF, Powerpoint, and so on.

How Accessible Is This Tool to All Users?

Accessibility for wikis is a mixed bag. Very well-known wikis, such as Wikipedia, run on common software by Mediawiki. In these cases, the wikis are screen reader–friendly and navigable by keyboards. Those with visual or mobility impairments are able to add text. Other wikis do not fare as well in accessibility testing, largely because they are not accessible using a screen reader, or because of content that other authors are able to add. Persons editing and adding to a wiki have to understand and respect accessibility guidelines for a wiki to stand a true test of accessibility. For example, you might have a wiki that is very accessible until someone adds random links or an image without an alt tag. An alt tag is a short text description of an image; the image might be of a horse and the screen reader reads "image of horse" if that is how you label the alt tag.

What Additional Vocabulary Do I Need to Know?

> *History*—a record within a wiki of who contributed what
>
> *Rollback*—the process of going back to a former version of the wiki, used when you need to review the history of changes or do not want to accept the latest changes

Can You Share a K–12 Example?

Your fifth-grade students are studying the early American colonies. You assign them the project of creating travel guides in small groups, but you hope they will work on this outside of class as well as in class. By creating a page on Google Docs for each group, you allow members to contribute from home. Google Docs is a collaborative tool that behaves like a wiki, allowing for multiple parties to edit a document. The students' page looks much like a word processing page, and it might resemble the one in Figure 12.1. Eventually, this page can be published for parents to view.

Can You Share a Higher Education Example?

You teach an instructional design course and want your class to brainstorm a list of criteria by which they would judge e-learning. You establish the wiki and instruct the students on how to use it. Each student makes a contribution, and the list grows. Later in the term, you are going to have small groups within separately organize an evaluative rubric from the contents. Figure 12.2 shows what the wiki looks like in its rough stages.

FIGURE 12.1. WIKI FOR STUDENT WORK CREATED USING GOOGLE DOCS

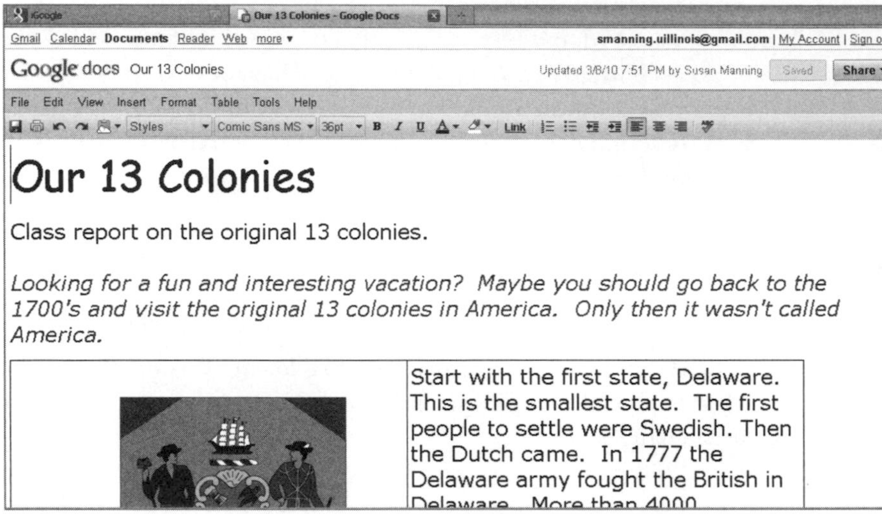

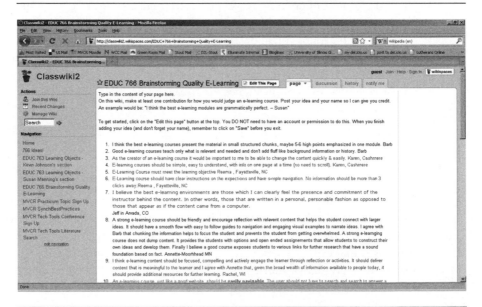

Used by permission.

FIGURE 12.2. CLASS WIKI CREATED USING WIKISPACES

Used by permission of Tangient LLC.

Where Can I Learn More?

To learn more about wikis, we recommend the following resources:

Richardson, W. (2008). *Blogs, wikis, podcasts, and other powerful Web tools for classrooms.* Thousand Oaks, CA: Corwin Press.

West, J., & West, M. (2008). *Using wikis for online collaboration.* San Francisco: Jossey-Bass.

Currently Available Tools

- Wikispaces at www.wikispaces.com/
- PBWorks at http://pbworks.com/
- Google Docs at http://docs.google.com/ (As a collaborative tool, this works a little differently from a wiki, but it is still relevant here in that it allows users to create Web pages others can edit.)

TABLE 12.1. DECISION-MAKING MATRIX—WIKIS

	Google Docs	Wikispaces
Type of Tool	Communication and collaboration Presentation of content	Communication and collaboration Presentation of content
Problem It Solves	This tool solves the problem of getting multiple users to add to a Web page. Users can also create spreadsheets and presentations collaboratively.	This tool solves the problem of getting multiple users to add to a Web page.
Cost	Free	Free
URL	http://docs.google.com/	www.wikispaces.com/
Description	After you create a free account, you can start creating pages, spreadsheets, or presentations and allow others to edit and make changes. You can determine whether editors need permission or whether the document is open. Documents can be downloaded in various formats. Editing by multiple parties can occur synchronously.	After you create a free account, you can start building Web pages and allow others to edit and make changes. You can determine whether editors need permission or whether the document is open.

(continued)

networks, and so on. Your pony will have a home in no time as long as you have established the network.

One of the features that makes microblogs very different from blogs is that almost all services allow readers to subscribe to messages received and sent as Short Message Service (SMS) text messages using their cell phones. Therefore, following someone via a microblog can be a cell phone experience or a Web-based experience. And remember the pony that needs a home? The information could be received by a network friend on his phone, but passed on to his cousin who is listed in his phone's contact list and who is not at all involved in microblogging. Microblogging can reach well beyond the Internet.

Finally, some microblogging tools allow users to "tag" or label their posts so that they are later searchable and retrievable. A common practice for a conference, for example, is for participants to comment on the conference with a common tag so that others (not in attendance) can follow along, access resources, and possibly participate in the conversation.

What Problem Does It Solve?

The key to using a microblog effectively is to remember that it reaches beyond the Internet and is both immediate and asynchronous. Thus, as a communication tool a microblog allows the author to publish ideas immediately to a far-reaching audience. A microblog could be used to make announcements, send reminders, or pose a question, because its forte is short chunks of information. On the one hand, it solves the problem of being able to reach your audience right away. On the other hand, because these posts are archived and may be searchable as a result of the tags or labels, microblog posts can serve as a repository of ideas on a common theme. The tool can be used to enable groups of students to react and respond to a subject or to collaborate in sharing resources and ideas.

Is This Something Instructors or Students Use?

Because a microblog could be viewed as an information source and as a venue for publishing, both instructors and students can use the tool. Either party can establish an account and create or read entries.

Is This Tool for the Novice, Intermediate, or Expert?

Following or writing a microblog on the computer is a novice-level activity. Synchronizing that microblog to your telephone texting service is probably also a novice-level activity. Using additional desktop-based software to sift through entries from multiple sources you follow may be an intermediate-level activity.

Is There Special Equipment or Software Needed?

No special equipment is needed, but you do need to access the Web based site provided by the vendor because it contains the programming code that allows you to write and to publish entries on a microblog with an RSS feed. There is an abundance of free Web-based tools available for this. Receiving messages through a cell phone is completely optional, but if you want to have messages go to your cell phone, you need one that can handle SMS messages.

What Are Some Cautions About This Tool?

Let's get the cell phone concern out of the way first. If you request to receive microblog entries on your cell phone, you will be charged by your provider in the same way you would to receive any other text message. Therefore, make sure you have unlimited texting service.

There is also a loss of privacy with this tool. When you establish an account and make your entries visible, anyone can begin to follow you. That includes people peddling services and products you may want no part of, including adult services. Furthermore, for some of the tools, there are add-on tools that allow users to track the location a post came from, resulting in a clear loss of privacy for the sender. The good news is that you are always informed of new followers and can block those people. That said, you need to be very careful when using this tool with a younger audience.

How Accessible Is This Tool to All Users?

Depending on which tool you select, microblogging can be very accessible. Twitter, for example, has a special version just for those with visual impairments. Many of the tools use forms that are well marked and accessible through a keyboard and not a pointer device.

What Additional Vocabulary Do I Need to Know?

Aggregator—a separate piece of software, such as Tweetdeck, that allows you to subscribe to and follow multiple RSS feeds from several different microblogs

Followers—people who subscribe to your microblogging activity

Hashtag or #—a user-created identifier used for classifying posts

Retweet (RT)— someone else's Twitter entry you have reposted so that your network can read it

Tweet—to send a message or post

Can You Share a K–12 Example?

You are a high school science teacher and wish to have several classes access identical assignments and resources. A newer product on the market, Edmodo, allows you to establish an account and have students microblog about class content. In this way, only students (and their parents) can access the site, and it is password protected. Figure 13.1 shows what this would look like from the teacher's perspective. You have several options in setting up the page. Having established groups according to the courses you teach, you use Edmodo to send assignments and announcements to students. In turn, students can microblog questions or comments about the postings. Alternately, your students from other classes might read postings you make of general science news and comment accordingly. You begin a scientific dialog across the school! These comments could be read online or sent to cell phones. Part of the appeal of a product like Edmodo is the privacy factor for students, because it has been developed with kids in mind. Also, similar to products used by adults, this site enables students (and parents) to subscribe to the site and receive information in text message form without having to log in.

FIGURE 13.1. EDMODO MICROBLOGGING ACCOUNT FOR A SCIENCE CLASS

Used by permission.

Can You Share a Higher Education Example?

You teach global political science, and your courses require students to follow current events and issues. In order to keep them in the political loop, you ask them to follow a major political party outside the United States or an academic who "tweets" about current issues on Twitter. Figure 13.2 shows one such Twitter page.

Where Can I Learn More?

To learn more about microblogs, we recommend the following resources:

> 7 things you should know about microblogging. (2009, July 7). *Educause.* Retrieved from www.educause.edu/Resources/7ThingsYouShould KnowAboutMicro/174629.
>
> McFedries, P. *Twitter: Tips, tricks, and tweets.* (2009). Indianapolis, IN: Wiley.

FIGURE 13.2. HIGHER EDUCATION FACULTY MEMBER'S PRESENCE ON TWITTER

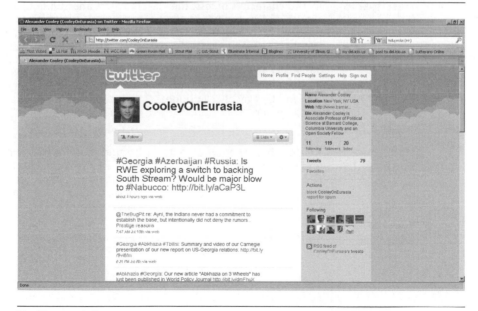

Used by permission.

Currently Available Tools

- Twitter at www.twitter.com
- Tumblr at www.tumblr.com
- Edmodo at www.edmodo.com

TABLE 13.1. DECISION-MAKING MATRIX—MICROBLOGS

	Twitter	Edmodo
Type of Tool	Communication and collaboration	Communication and collaboration
Problem It Solves	This tool solves the problem of busy students not getting important information. It allows an instructor to make almost immediate announcements that students can access via Web or cell phone.	This tool solves a communication problem for instructors in that it provides a safe environment for students to leave short comments on various topics, viewable to the class. The instructor can also make announcements.
Cost	Free	Free
URL	www.twitter.com	www.edmodo.com
Description	In 140 characters or less, the sender creates a message and posts on his or her Twitter site. Receivers subscribe to the feed so that they are informed whenever a new post is available. Users can read and respond by way of cell phone or computer.	Teachers and students can maintain a microblog for discussions and assignments. There are other tools within the products that include polls and calendars, and users have the ability to have messages sent to their cell phones via SMS text messaging.
Platform	Web	Web
Best Used For	Making short announcements and sharing class resources	Getting students to comment on assignments and each other's ideas, and making short announcements and sharing class resources
Level of Expertise	*Teacher:* Basic *Student:* Basic	*Teacher:* Basic *Student:* Basic

TABLE 13.1. (*continued*)

	Twitter	Edmodo
Cautions	This is a public venue. Strange people might start to "follow" you. Also, if you subscribe via cell phone, make sure you have an unlimited texting plan!	There are none. Because this company specifically works with K–12 educators, it has many safeguards built in. However, if you or students subscribe via cell phone, make sure you have an unlimited texting plan!
Overcoming Cautions	Use this tool only with adult students, not children.	This tool is specifically developed with the K–12 audience in mind; therefore, Edmodo has already addressed any potential privacy issues.
Accessibility Concerns	This tool is fully accessible. To help those with visual impairments, consult www.accessibletwitter.com/.	According to developers, the product accommodates screen readers well, although keyboard shortcuts have not yet been developed.
Special Equipment	None	None
Additional Vocabulary	*Tweet, hashtag, followers, aggregator*	None
Training and Resources	http://twitter.com/help/start	www.edmodo.com/guide/

CHAPTER FOURTEEN

WEB CONFERENCING

In the song "Welcome to the Future," popular country music star Brad Paisley sings about of some of the changes he has witnessed in his life, including the ability to video chat with a company on another continent. Technology is no longer exclusive to Fortune 500 companies, but rather is available and accessible to everyone, including teachers, for establishing businesses and maintaining communication. In this chapter, we look at how Web conferencing can be used in an educational context.

What Is the Tool?

A Web conferencing tool combines several features that allow for voice, video, and text to be shared in real time. A participant in a Web conference may see the speakers through a video feed, hear the audio, view slides or images, and chat with fellow participants. The participant may also be asked to answer polls, write on a whiteboard, or view shared applications. With many Web conferencing tools, meetings can be recorded for later playback. The instructor can determine how many of these features to use at any given time.

What Problem Does It Solve?

Students who enroll in online courses sometimes report feeling disconnected or socially isolated. They long to feel part of the class or connected to the instructor and their peers. Web conferencing most closely approximates the sense of "being there" for distance learners. Participants engage in authentic communication because Web conferencing allows them to share video, audio, and images in real time. In regard to instruction, Web conferencing mimics what happens in a typical classroom by invoking a multisensory experience.

Is This Something Instructors or Students Use?

Typically, instructors initiate Web conferencing sessions that students attend. In some adult education contexts, students might meet independent of the instructor in a Web conferencing tool.

Is This Tool for the Novice, Intermediate, or Expert?

Web conferencing is a more sophisticated instructional activity, requiring intermediate skills to master the combination of features. As with many tools, using Web conferencing products requires some additional training in pedagogy as well as in knowing which buttons to push. Setting up and administrating a Web conferencing tool are possibly advanced skills, but most instructors would not need to do that for themselves.

Is There Special Equipment or Software Needed?

First we need to differentiate between browser-based and client-based Web conferencing products. With a browser-based product, the conference is contained within your regular browser; no special download is required. With a client-based product, you may need to download a small program in order to access the conference. Institutions may view some of these synchronous tools as security threats, and firewalls may prevent the products from loading. If you are attempting to use a client-based Web conferencing product from your office or classroom at school, discuss this with your information technology personnel.

Aside from software, users need some equipment if they are to fully participate. To hear the audio, a user needs a headset or speakers connected to the computer. To speak to other parties in the conference, the user needs a microphone. To show his or her face in video, the user needs a webcam.

What Are Some Cautions About This Tool?

There are a few cautions with this tool, mainly related to the connectivity and hardware needs. Some Web conferencing companies specifically state that their products run on low bandwidth and work with slower Internet connections, but the more tools and features you add, the more likely it is that you will have difficulty. The video feed might be unrecognizable, or audio could cut in and out. Students with older machines and slower processors may have difficulty maintaining a connection.

Although not a caution, per se, the most challenging aspect of using a Web conferencing tool seems to be scheduling! With adult learners, in particular, finding a time when all parties are available requires quite a bit of coordination. For this reason, we strongly encourage faculty who require synchronous sessions to make this known to students prior to enrollment. Further help with scheduling can be found in Chapter Four, Scheduling Tools.

Privacy is not a particular concern. With younger learners, Web conferencing is always teacher controlled, and conferences are typically established with password-required log-ins. For adults, even when Web conferencing is used by groups of students for group projects, sessions are closed to outsiders.

How Accessible Is This Tool to All Users?

Accessibility tests reveal mixed results for Web conferencing products. As you might expect, you get what you pay for. The more expensive products have taken steps to allow for greater accessibility. This includes closed-captioning, screen-reader accessibility, and shortcut keys. Free products may not have these same accommodations, and may not be accessible to users with disabilities.

What Additional Vocabulary Do I Need to Know?

Synchronous—occurring in real time

Webcam—a small video device that sends video images

Whiteboard—a feature that allows a conference participant to write on a virtual screen, for example when working through a math problem or typing a phrase

Can You Share a K–12 Example?

You teach in a virtual school. Students often work independently on assignments, but you also call them together for additional lessons and community building.

FIGURE 14.1. VIRTUAL ELEMENTARY SCHOOL CLASS MEETING

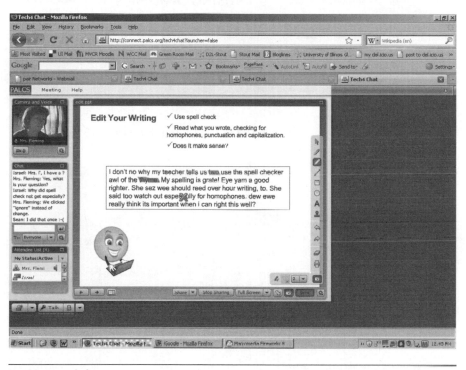

Used by permission.

Figure 14.1 shows one teacher's activities as she reviews grammar with her class in Adobe Connect. They can see her and talk to her using microphones. When they turn on their cameras, they can see and talk to each other, too. They can also write on the whiteboard and manipulate objects the teacher places there.

Can You Share a Higher Education Example?

You teach an eight-week English course using an asynchronous platform. However, every week during in the term, you offer optional Web conferencing sessions to answer questions about the course material and explain upcoming assignments. Students can watch you talk to them using a webcam and can chat on the side. The session is recorded so that students who cannot attend still have access to the information. Figure 14.2 shows an example of such a meeting.

FIGURE 14.2. CLASS MEETING FOR AN ONLINE COURSE USING DIMDIM

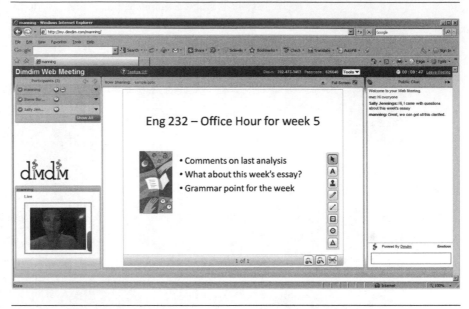

Used by permission.

Where Can I Learn More?

Without a doubt the best resource for using a synchronous web conferencing tool is

Finkelstein, J. (2006). *Learning in real time.* San Francisco: Jossey-Bass.

Currently Available Tools

- Elluminate at http://elluminate.com/
- Adobe Connect at www.adobe.com/products/acrobatconnectpro/
- Dimdim at http://www.dimdim.com/solutions/dimdim_education.html
- Vyew at www.adobe.com/products/acrobatconnectpro/

TABLE 14.1. DECISION-MAKING MATRIX—WEB CONFERENCING

	Adobe Connect	Dimdim
Type of Tool	Communication and collaboration Presentation of content	Communication and collaboration Presentation of content
Problem It Solves	Students sometimes feel disconnected from their instructor or classmates. This tool brings people together. It combines voice communication and video or slides for real-time conferencing. It's as close to being in the same room as you can come online.	Students sometimes feel disconnected from their instructor or classmates. This tool brings people together. It combines voice communication and video or slides for real-time conferencing. It's as close to being in the same room as you can come online.
Cost	Expensive	Free or inexpensive
URL	www.adobe.com/products/acrobatconnectpro/	www.dimdim.com/
Description	As a Web conferencing tool, Adobe Connect allows you to broadcast slides or a whiteboard while talking with an audience. You can also share video, your computer screen, or a Web site. Polls and chats are additional features that enhance audience interaction.	As a Web conferencing tool, Dimdim allows you to broadcast slides or a whiteboard while talking with an audience. You can also share video, your computer screen, or a Web site. Meetings can be recorded. There is a free version as well as a commercial product.
Platform	Web	Web
Best Used For	Situations in which you want to communicate in real time with more than just voice	Situations in which you want to communicate in real time with more than just voice
Level of Expertise	*Teacher:* Intermediate *Student:* Basic	*Teacher:* Intermediate *Student:* Basic
Cautions	See notes about accessibility. Also, this product requires a certain level of bandwidth and a decent Internet connection in terms of speed. It also requires a Flash player to be installed.	See notes about accessibility. Also, this product requires a certain level of bandwidth and a decent Internet connection in terms of speed.
Overcoming Cautions	Make sure users work through a "technical check" prior to the first meeting. That gives them time to download and install any additional updates they may need.	Make sure users work through a "technical check" prior to the first meeting.

(continued)

TABLE 14.1. (*continued*)

	Adobe Connect	Dimdim
Accessibility Concerns	Adobe runs on a Flash-based system, and some users report difficulties. For those with visual disabilities who use screen readers, menu navigation, keyboard shortcuts, and tab navigation are available. For those with hearing disabilities, closed-captioning can be added to the platform, but that requires hiring someone to do this.	This particular product does not provide a lot of accessibility information. It is free, after all. If you have students with visual impairments who use screen readers, this might not be a good product to select. Research this carefully. You also need to consider whether closed-captioning could work with the product for those who are hearing impaired.
Special Equipment	Headset or microphone and speakers	Headset or microphone and speakers
Additional Vocabulary	*Synchronous, webcam, whiteboard*	*Synchronous, webcam, whiteboard*
Training and Resources	www.adobe.com/support/ connect/	http://onlinehelp.dimdim.com/

PART FOUR

TOOLS TO PRESENT CONTENT

We all have different ways of learning. Some of us prefer reading information, whereas others prefer listening to presentations. Some even prefer to touch and manipulate things as a way of understanding. As an instructor, it is important to recognize these differences and incorporate a variety of presentation methods in a course as a way of engaging all students. By giving students choices on how they wish to demonstrate their understanding of the subject matter and providing them with the proper tools, you create an atmosphere that encourages learning and increases success.

You can present subject matter, or the content of your course, in many different ways. Whether you create the information to share with the students or vice versa, content can be presented using text, still images, audio, video, or any combination of these. Part Four focuses on many of these tools along with their benefits and challenges. As we introduce these tools, keep in mind the principle of Universal Design: when content is presented in a way that addresses learners with different needs (for example, students who are blind or hearing impaired, or those with learning disabilities) it benefits everyone. For example, when creating audio files, it is always important to include a text-based transcript for students who may be deaf or hard of hearing. By having the transcript, you are also meeting the learning needs of those who may be able to hear but prefer to read content as oppose to listen to it.

CHAPTER FIFTEEN

AUDIO

Audio and the power of the human voice humanize the learning experience, especially for students at a distance who may feel a little more disconnected from the instructor and their peers. There are a number of tools that allow instructors and students to create narrations or music files. Audio can be used to introduce a new module or learning unit, compare musical notes, critique pronunciation, and encourage dialogue. In this chapter, we focus on the tools used to create an audio file.

Single Audio Files Versus Podcasts

Depending on your instructional goals, you may use audio only once; students simply download a file to their computers from a link you have provided. Once they have downloaded the file, they open the file in a common audio player, such as Windows Media Player or iTunes, listen to the file, and perhaps store it for review later. However, as an instructor, you may also choose to present audio content on a more consistent basis. In that case, you would want to create a system in which you could post your audio files on the Web and create what is known as a Really Simple Syndication (RSS) feed. Students could then subscribe to your RSS feed and be notified of new audio files as you create them. This is known as podcasting.

Podcasts are used in academic environments in which content is presented on a regular basis. For example, an instructor may wish to post a weekly interview with a professional in the field. The instructor will conduct the interviews, record them using an audio-recording tool, and then upload them to a site where they are tagged and formatted as podcast episodes. Students can either visit the Web site every week by manual navigation or set up RSS readers to automatically check whether new content is available and, if so, download the new content directly.

What Is the Tool?

When we use the phrase *audio tools*, we are referring to tools to create, save, or play audio-only files. Most computers come with an application that allows you to listen to audio files, such as iTunes (www.apple.com/itunes/), Windows Media Player (www.microsoft.com/windows/windowsmedia/player/default.aspx), or RealPlayer (www.real.com/). These applications are free for listening, but often require purchasing an upgrade in order to create content. Therefore, we recommend that you conduct additional research before spending money on features that other free applications may include.

What Problem Does It Solve?

Audio solves a couple of problems related to pedagogy. First and foremost, using audio is a way for instructors to present content that can only come in audio format, such as music, spoken language, and sound effects. Can you imagine a Spanish class with no listening component or a music appreciation class with no sonatas? Second, depending on your instructional objectives, audio tools can reduce transactional distance by giving online students a voice to place with your name and image (assuming you post a picture in the virtual classroom), or with those of any other student with whom they exchange audio.

Is This Something Instructors or Students Use?

Both instructors and students can use this tool. Not only can instructors create and share files related to course content but also students can do the same to demonstrate understanding of course material.

Is This Tool for the Novice, Intermediate, or Expert?

A novice user can learn how to record audio in a fairly short amount of time. However, audio files can be saved (rendered) in multiple formats depending on how they will be delivered. The file's type affects its size and sound quality, and can restrict access to users by requiring specific software to play it. How a user is going to deliver the content is also an important part of determining the level of experience a user needs. If a user is going to simply upload the file to a course management system or send it attached to an e-mail, then the competency requirements are minimal. However, if the user is planning to stream the file over the Internet, which means delivering media in a way that allows others to listen to the file without having to download it directly to their computers, the user must understand streaming technologies and have access to the proper hardware and software.

Is There Special Equipment or Software Needed?

As mentioned earlier, most computers come with applications that allow you to listen to audio files. Therefore, let's consider what you need to *produce* an audio file. Along with software, you must have a microphone. To be honest, many of the recordings we create are recorded using inexpensive microphones that you can purchase at almost any technology or office-product retailer for less than twenty-five dollars. If you have a quiet place with little background noise, these microphones are fine.

There are two types of microphones: unidirectional and multidirectional. Unidirectional microphones require that sound enter from one direction, which is good for single-person or instrumental recording. However, if the sounds of the surrounding environment are important to your recording, look for a multidirectional microphone, which allows noise to enter from multiple directions.

You will also need software to capture the audio, edit the recording, and produce it (save it in the format you want). There are very expensive products available, but there are also free products that are marvelous. Many audio producers know and trust Audacity, a free product. Mac users may experiment with GarageBand.

Once you have created the audio files, you can use them as is or add them to other media, such as PowerPoint slide presentations. You can use products like SlideShare (www.slideshare.net) to distribute narrated slide shows over the Internet.

What Are Some Cautions About This Tool?

Although this is not a caution, we commonly hear that the most difficult aspect of creating audio is getting over the dislike of hearing your own voice upon playback. This is common for anyone in the recording business. With time, this fear goes away, and the number of takes to make a recording diminishes.

The second caution with audio files is the time it takes to edit in postproduction. Depending on what you are doing, postproduction can either be quick or take a very long time. There are times when we don't care as much about our "ums" and "ahs." For example, when providing students with verbal feedback about an assignment, we will often hit the record button, record our comments, and send it to the respective students without regard to editing. However, when Susan records for her professional podcast, postproduction requires a lot of a producer's time to edit sound quality, remove noise, render the file, and post it to the Web.

How Accessible Is This Tool to All Users?

Whenever using audio to deliver content, it's important to save the file in a common file format that can be played by multiple players and to make available a text-based transcript. This allows users to choose tools with which they are most familiar, and gives them the opportunity to read the information rather than listen to it.

When asking students to create content using audio, a text-based alternative may be needed for students unable to create such files (students who are deaf, for example). If students are expected to share their work with peers, it's also important that their work be accompanied by text-based transcripts or narratives explaining the content.

What Additional Vocabulary Do I Need to Know?

Multitrack—having multiple tracks that compress into one file when rendered

Omnidirectional microphone—a recording device that picks up environmental noise from multiple directions

Podcasts—audio files saved to a Web site using RSS technologies that allow users to subscribe to a syndication feed and be automatically notified when new content is available

Really Simple Syndication (RSS)—technology that allows users to subscribe to a syndicated feed on the Web and be notified when new content is available

Rendering—the act of saving an audio or video file in a specific format so that it can be accessed by the intended audience using a variety of audio and video players

Streaming—delivering media via the Internet in a way that allows users to listen to the files without having to download them directly to their computers

Unidirectional microphone—a recording device that requires sound to enter from one direction, good for single-person or instrumental recording

Can You Share a K–12 Example?

Parents sometimes feel distant from their child's elementary school teacher. Imagine you are an instructor creating a weekly or biweekly audio newsletter for students and parents. Each audio announcement includes a recap of the previous week's accomplishments and an overview of the upcoming week's content. You could also share important school and class events, such as field trips and the dates and times for your parent-teacher conferences. Announcements also encourage parent participation by encouraging classroom visits or by sharing contact information. Depending on the instructor's understanding of the technology, the newsletter could either be available for manual download from the instructor's Web site or set up as a podcast to which parents could subscribe to receive updates automatically when new announcements are posted. A program for podcasting for Mac users is GarageBand, which comes free on all Macs.

Can You Share a Higher Education Example?

You are an English as a Second Language (ESL) instructor at a local community college working in a blended classroom environment. Half of the class time is spent in a traditional brick-and-mortar classroom and the other half is spent online. You use Audacity to create audio files of yourself recording each week's vocabulary words so that students can hear you pronounce each word and use it in a sentence. Students would have access to these recordings whenever they wanted, and class time could be spent reinforcing the audio content through discussion and dialogue.

In a blended environment, you could easily take time out of your schedule to teach students how to use Audacity themselves so that they could record their own assignments using the same vocabulary. Audacity is a free audio editor that is easy to use and allows multitrack recording. With multitrack recording, you can record multiple voices or background sounds separately and then combine them on one recording. For example, if you want background music that fades to you speaking, your voice could be on one track and the background music on another. You could then adjust each track's place on the timeline as well as the independent volume levels. Once you have completed a recording, Audacity

FIGURE 15.1. VOCABULARY ASSIGNMENT BEING RECORDED IN AUDACITY

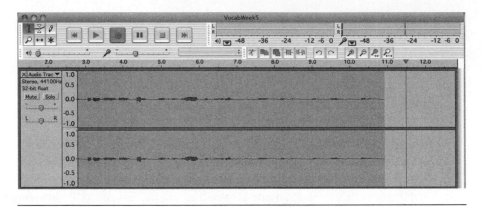

Used by permission.

allows you to use a LAME encoder to export the final product as an MP3 file, which is a universal audio file recognized by most media players.

Students could tell stories using the vocabulary words and record their stories for instructor review and to share with the rest of the class. This provides a very appropriate medium for students to demonstrate their language abilities and progress. Figure 15.1 illustrates the recording interface users see when recording audio files with Audacity.

Where Can I Learn More?

To learn more about podcasting or incorporating media into your classroom, we recommend the following resources:

Morris, T., Tomasi, C., Terra, E., & Steppe, K. (2008). *Podcasting for dummies* (2nd ed.). Hoboken, NJ: Wiley.

Smaldino, S. E., & Lowther, D. L. (2007). *Instructional technology and media for learning* (9th ed.). Upper Saddle River, NJ: Prentice Hall.

Currently Available Tools

- Audacity at http://audacity.sourceforge.net
- GarageBand at www.apple.com/ilife/garageband/
- Propaganda at www.makepropaganda.com/

TABLE 15.1. DECISION-MAKING MATRIX—AUDIO

	GarageBand	Audacity
Type of Tool	Communication and collaboration Presentation of content	Communication and collaboration Presentation of content
Problem It Solves	This tool helps humanize the learning experience for distance learners and meets instructional objectives pertaining to students' abilities to listen and speak. By hearing an instructor's voice, or by being able to submit assignments using their own voices, students can feel more connected to their distant instructor and peers.	This tool helps humanize the learning experience for distance learners and meets instructional objectives pertaining to students' abilities to listen and speak.
Cost	Free	Free
URL	www.apple.com/ilife/ garageband/	http://audacity.sourceforge.net/
Description	GarageBand is an easy to use, multitrack audio editing application that comes free with all Mac computers.	Audacity is an open-source, multitrack audio tool that is easy to use for editing audio and exporting the files to universal formats.
Platform	Mac	Web
Example (URL)	www.apple.com/ilife/ garageband/	http://kevin.thecuttinged.com/ education/nova/edd8008/ projects.php
Best Used For	Sharing content that is optimally delivered using audio, such as language, music, instructor announcements, and more	Sharing content that is optimally delivered using audio, such as language, music, instructor announcements, and more
Level of Expertise	*Teacher:* Intermediate *Student:* Basic	*Teacher:* Intermediate *Student:* Basic
Cautions	The learning curve is not that steep, but it will take some time to really learn how to use the product.	Audacity is an open-source technology, so its existence relies on a community of volunteers to keep it up and running. Users must have a basic understanding of multi-track audio-recording tools. Users must also download and install the free LAME MP3 encoding software.

(continued)

TABLE 15.1. (*continued*)

	GarageBand	Audacity
Overcoming Cautions	Users can access the training tutorials or purchase Mac 1:1 training support in their stores to learn how to use the product.	Students can be directed to Audacity's documentation Web site (http://audacity.sourceforge .net/help/documentation) for support. The instructor can develop additional support materials and, when possible, demonstrate how to install and use the program in a live, synchronous environment, such as a computer lab or Web conference.
Accessibility Concerns	Overall, Mac products rate high in terms of accessibility. Their operating system and base programs, including GarageBand, come with important assistance for multiple users, such as magnified text, screen-reader capabilities, and so on.	The initial install process may be a little difficult for some users. However, the Audacity community has made purposeful efforts to make the interface accessible for users with screen readers.
Special Equipment	Microphone for recording and speakers for playback	Microphone, speakers for playback, and free LAME MP3 encoding plug-in for saving files in the MP3 format

Additional Vocabulary	*Multitrack*—having multiple tracks that compress into one file when rendered
	Omnidirectional microphone—a recording device that picks up environmental noise from multiple directions
	Podcasts—audio files saved to a Web site using RSS technologies that allow users to subscribe to a syndication feed and be automatically notified when new content is available
	Really Simple Syndication (RSS)—technology that allows users to subscribe to a syndicated feed on the Web and be notified when new content is available
	Rendering—the act of saving an audio or video file in a specific format so that it can be accessed by the intended audience using a variety of audio and video players
	Streaming—delivering media via the Internet in a way that allows users to listen to the files without having to download them directly to their computers
	Unidirectional microphone—a recording device that requires sound to enter from one direction, good for single-person or instrumental recording

Training and Resources	www.apple.com/ilife/tutorials/ #garageband	http://audacity.sourceforge.net/ help/documentation

CHAPTER SIXTEEN

VIDEO

For years educators have used video to deliver course content. Whether it is a documentary on the effects of greenhouse gases, a movie version of a recently read book, or Sesame Street, video is used to encourage education through the combined use of visual effects, dialogue, demonstration, and, most recently, viewer interaction. Like with audio, there are tools to both view video and create it. Most computers come with the necessary tools to view video, and with the popularity of hosting services like YouTube and the prevalence of personal cameras, webcams, and cell phones, video is now easier than ever to create. This chapter explores the benefits and challenges for both instructors and students of using video tools to edit content-based video files.

Before we talk about the tools used to edit video, indulge us for just a moment as we briefly discuss video capturing. Video capturing refers to recording moving objects. For our purposes, this can either be in the form of live audiences, such as one of you interviewing a professional in the field as a way of providing students with a virtual guest lecture, or it can also mean capturing video that shows what is happening on your screen in order to demonstrate how to complete specific tasks within a particular application, such as Microsoft Word (see Chapter Seventeen, Screencasting, for more information). For this chapter, we'll focus on quick videos you can record using live actors in order to help personalize the learning experience of your students. For this purpose, quick videos captured with a webcam or modern-day mobile phone will most likely do the trick. These devices keep video files small, and users are usually somewhat familiar with how to use them. There are several compact models on the market that cost as little as $49.99 and plug directly into your computer for downloading the video files to your hard drive. Some of the new computers even have webcams built into the fronts of their monitors, keeping you from having to worry about external devices.

For more extensive video capturing, an instructor may consider using a personal video camera or a still camera with a video option. These cameras tend to produce higher-quality video files with better audio. These cameras are good for longer videos in which visual content is important to the instructional objectives. For example, a video that demonstrates how to conduct a standard medical exam to determine the difference between possible cancer spots and ordinary freckles will require clear views of the exam process with close-ups on the skin.

After capturing the video, editing is necessary for removing all the extra footage, removing background noises, and adding background music if desired. The editing can be as simple or as complex as a user wishes it to be. To really understand video editing takes a lot of time and practice. This chapter focuses on the more entry-level editing that can be completed using some of the free or inexpensive editing tools currently available. Once the video is captured and edited, uploading the video to your course management system or such a service as YouTube will allow you to distribute the content to your students.

As always, it's important to remember Universal Design and accessibility when creating course content. Don't forget to create transcripts for all videos, or choose a service that allows you to add closed-captioning. A quick tip for those who will be recording live actors: develop a script of what actors will say ahead of time and use that script as the transcript for your students.

What Is the Tool?

In a perfect world, we would all be able to capture a perfect video without "ums" and "ahs," and we would be able to get everything we needed in one shoot. Well, none of us are perfect, and we are often required to record the same shot multiple times and then paste the pieces together later. Therefore, once the video is captured, it's time for editing before distribution. The tools used to edit videos are the true focus of this chapter.

The word *video* refers to moving images with sound. Videos can be saved to digital files and then distributed and viewed over the Internet. Distribution can be through either a static link that requires students to download the video to their computers or a streaming service that allows students to watch the video directly on the Web without downloading. Videos can also be created like podcasts:

visitors to your site can subscribe to a feed that notifies them when new videos have been added. These are called vodcasts, short for video podcasts.

What Problem Does It Solve?

There are some things that are best seen to be understood or appreciated, such as a chemical reaction or the correct position for bowing a cello or the technique for whipping cream. Video solves the problem of demonstrating process and reactions in real time. In this manner, video can also serve as a way for you to give students a virtual experience they couldn't otherwise have. For example, you could provide students with a virtual tour of the ocean floor in an oceanography course—something difficult for the average midwestern student to experience for him- or herself. Diving in local lakes and ponds just isn't the same.

Also, depending on your instructional objectives, video can reduce transactional distance by giving distance students an image and voice to place with your written presence.

Is This Something Instructors or Students Use?

Both instructors and students can create and distribute video. Video can be used for a variety of pedagogical purposes, whereby students can learn from watching or can demonstrate their abilities by creating their own video files. For example, we know of a distance course that teaches introduction to dance in which students watch videos on dance steps and then actually record themselves dancing for the instructor to review.

Is This Tool for the Novice, Intermediate, or Expert?

Creating simple videos by using digital cameras or mobile phones requires novice-level skills. However, more extensive video capturing and editing can necessitate intermediate- or expert-level skills. For example, a project with transitions and titles that a student completes for a film course may require more time and technical competencies than does a simple, thirty-second welcome video from the instructor that needs no edits or transitions.

Is There Special Equipment or Software Needed?

Most computers come with applications that allow you to view video files. Some videos viewed online only require a Web browser, such as Internet Explorer or Safari, and a connection to the Internet. Creating video, however, requires a video-capturing device, such as a webcam or video camera. If the video includes voice-audio, then a microphone is also required (it may be built into the camera).

Once the video has been captured, if the content creator would like to add background sounds, edit video transitions, or improve the audio quality, video-editing software is required. Both Macs and Windows machines have free video-editing software available that helps even a beginner edit videos like a pro. On Windows machines there is Movie Maker, and on Macs there are iMovie and iDVD for those wishing to publish their finished products onto DVDs. iMovie and iDVD come preinstalled on all Mac machines. Movie Maker was preinstalled on Windows machines until Windows 7 was released. It can now be downloaded for free from Microsoft's Web site.

What Are Some Cautions About This Tool?

The biggest caution when incorporating self-produced videos into your curriculum is to be aware of the time it takes to complete the full production process. With minimal knowledge and no editing, a video can take as little as ten or fifteen minutes to shoot and upload to the Web. However, creating only ten minutes of high-quality video can take up to one hundred hours. This is very important to keep in mind when planning a video project or expecting students to create video in your classroom. Having students capture video is a wonderful way of asking them to demonstrate their skills, but the time it takes for students to complete the task should be calculated into the overall curriculum expectations pertaining to time-on-task. Many instructors do not do this and expect students to create video while managing several other course tasks, which requires full-time hours—something rarely available to all students.

Another caution centers on the resources available. Students who are taking a face-to-face class in which all students are sitting in front of computers, have access to the same software, and are provided with instruction specific to that software may be able to accomplish more in less time than students who are working from a distance, use different computers, and have access to different resources. When expecting students to create video, the more resources complementing the variety of tools the better. Creating and locating these resources on the Web can also be time-consuming.

How Accessible Is This Tool to All Users?

Although videos can be a great resource, they are pointless if they are not accessible to your audience. Like with audio files, it is important that a video either be captioned or be accompanied by a transcript. Using closed-captioning means that words display on the screen as they are being said. Closed-captioning also includes descriptive text of background sounds, such as applause or music. It requires special software that is usually expensive and difficult to quickly learn to use. However, YouTube now offers a free closed-captioning service for videos that you distribute on their site (see http://www.youtube.com/t/captions_about). There are also commercial companies that will add captions to videos for a fee. This can cost as much as ten dollars per minute of video.

Some students (for example, those who are blind) may need a text-based alternative to be able to produce video files. If students are expected to share their work with peers, it's also important that their work be accompanied by text-based transcripts or narratives explaining the content.

What Additional Vocabulary Do I Need to Know?

Closed Captioning—adding narrative and descriptive text to videos that display in a timely manner relative to what is happening on the screen

Capturing—the act of using a recording device to record moving objects, whether live actors or actions on a computer screen

Editing—cleaning up irregularities and adding titles, subtitles, and credits

Multitrack—having multiple tracks that compress into one file when rendered

Rendering   the act of saving an audio or video file in a specific format so that it can be accessed by the intended audience using a variety of audio and video players

Vodcast—videos created and shared via the Web using syndication feeds so that subscribers can be notified of new posts when available

Can You Share a K–12 Example?

Let's assume that you are a fifth-grade teacher. Your class is learning about the U.S. presidents. Students would be broken up into groups, and each group is assigned a president to study. Each group is also responsible for creating a campaign video for their respective president. They would develop a storyboard regarding the campaign and its overall message, assigning a member to "act" as the president, a cameraperson, and a production crew. With proper training and supervision, students would storyboard their production shoot and use editing software, such as iMovie, to add titles and transitions. The final products would be privately shared with parents on such a service as YouTube. To add a little interaction, parents would also use the comment feature on YouTube to submit time-period-specific questions that the groups would research and respond to. Another great benefit of this assignment is that students can use this experience to explore the financial difference between campaigning in the past and campaigning now. You could also engage students in discussions about how video changes the campaign dynamics. For example, students could explore whether or not a president seen in a wheelchair would have been elected if he had been shown on air at the time of election.

Can You Share a Higher Education Example?

Suppose as a marketing course instructor, you want your students to analyze the similarities and differences in the commercials during the Super Bowl. You would locate the commercials online and provide links to them for review by the class. Students would be responsible for reviewing each commercial, and then

FIGURE 16.1. INSTRUCTOR PLAYLIST OF VIDEOS FOR STUDENTS TO WATCH ON YOUTUBE

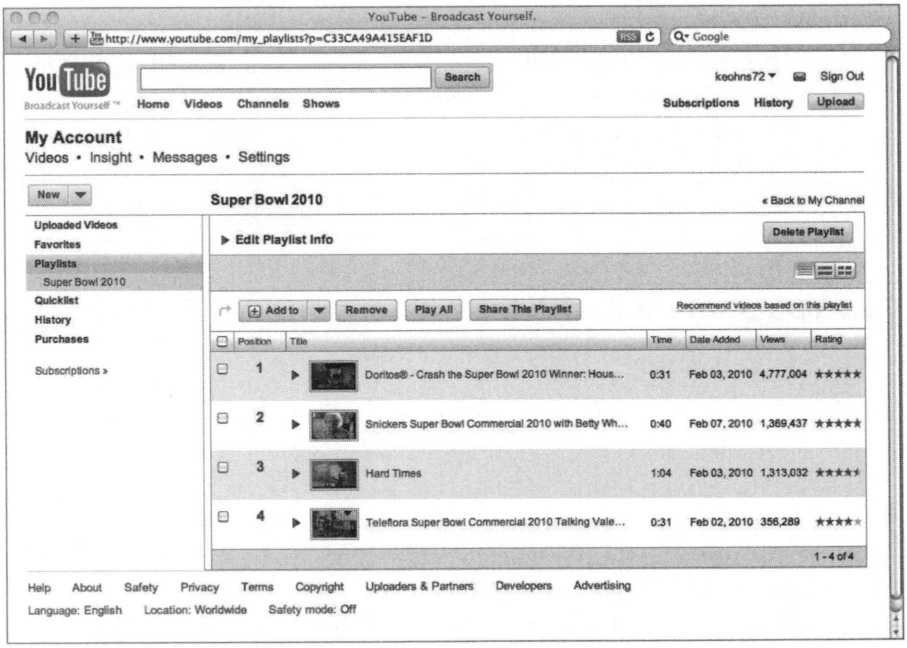

Used by permission.

would participate in a discussion on how the commercials are similar and how they are different based on strategies discussed throughout the course of the class. To help in the analysis process, students could use comments shared within each video's discussion forum to support their arguments about how effective the commercial was. Figure 16.1 illustrates an example playlist page in YouTube, which you could create using your free YouTube account to share specific videos with students based on the given assignment.

Where Can I Learn More?

To learn more about video creation and distribution, we recommend the following resources:

Bourne, J., & Burstein, D. (2008). *Web video: Making it great, getting it noticed.* Berkeley, CA: Peachpit Press.

Smaldino, S. E., & Lowther, D. L. (2007). *Instructional technology and media for learning* (9th ed.). Upper Saddle River, NJ: Prentice Hall.

Currently Available Tools

Creating Video
- iMovie at www.apple.com/ilife/imovie/
- iDVD at www.apple.com/ilife/idvd/
- Windows Live Movie Maker at http://download.live.com/moviemaker

Distributing Video
- YouTube at www.youtube.com
- TeacherTube at www.teachertube.com
- Scholastic TeacherShare at http://teachershare.scholastic.com/

TABLE 16.1. DECISION-MAKING MATRIX—VIDEO

	iMovie	YouTube
Type of Tool	Presentation of content	Presentation of content
Problem It Solves	This tool helps humanize the learning experience for distance learners and meets instructional objectives pertaining to content best delivered using visual effects, audio, or a combination of the two. Videos with the instructor can help students feel better connected, while visual learners also benefit by receiving content in the preferred medium.	This tool helps humanize the learning experience for distance learners and meets instructional objectives pertaining to content best delivered using visual effects, audio, or a combination of the two. Videos with the instructor can help students feel better connected, while visual learners also benefit by receiving content in the preferred medium.
Cost	Free	Free
URL	www.apple.com/ilife/imovie/	http://youtube.com
Description	The iMovie application is included with the iLife suite, which comes free with new Macs. It allows users to import, edit, and share video files.	YouTube is a Web-based video distribution site where users can upload videos to the site and share them publicly or privately with other Internet users.
Platform	Mac	Web
Best Used For	Creating and sharing content that is optimally delivered using video, such as an instructor's welcome message, video productions, and more	Creating and sharing content that is optimally delivered using video, such as an instructor's welcome message, video productions, and more
Level of Expertise	*Teacher:* Intermediate *Student:* Intermediate	*Teacher:* Basic *Student:* Basic
Cautions	iMovie only comes with Mac computers and requires some introduction for those unfamiliar with video production. Video editing in general can take time; therefore, instructional objectives must really warrant students' creating content in video format. Due to the specific nature of their projects, students will not be able to rely on technical support for help. They will need to turn to their instructor.	When working with video on a public site, you have to be concerned about copyright, and must be aware that some links may die over time.

TABLE 16.1. (*continued*)

	iMovie	YouTube
Overcoming Cautions	Apple provides support videos and additional help documentation on the application's Web site. Students may also choose to use products with which they are more familiar or, with your permission, may submit the assignment in a text-based format instead. You can demonstrate the use of iMovie in a synchronous environment as a way of providing students with an introduction to the application.	Try to use videos in which the content is obviously original and belongs to the content creator. Otherwise, you risk violating copyright laws and videos being taken down quickly by YouTube administration, leaving you to search for other videos to use in your class. Also, check links before providing them for your students, and be prepared to find additional videos if and when links die. Finally, when asking students to post to YouTube, give them the option of making their content private and inviting you to watch their videos via links sent over e-mail.
Accessibility Concerns	Apple has a public statement about its commitment to accessibility. Apple's operating system has accessibility features built into all its native applications, including iMovie. Features include screen magnification, voice-over options, and an alternative, more simplified user interface.	When using existing content out on the Web, there is no guarantee that the content is accessible by multiple users with different learning needs and technological skills. Be prepared to find alternative ways to meet your learning objectives.
Special Equipment	Webcam, video camera, or other video recording device; microphone for voice recording; speakers for playback	Speakers for playback

(continued)

TABLE 16.1. (*continued*)

	iMovie	YouTube
Additional Vocabulary	*Closed Captioning*—adding narrative and descriptive text to videos that display in a timely manner relative to what is happening on the screen *Capturing*—using a recording device to record moving objects, whether live actors or actions on a computer screen *Editing*—cleaning up irregularities and adding titles, subtitles, and credits *Multitrack*—having multiple tracks that compress into one file when rendered *Rendering*—saving an audio or video file in a specific format so that it can be accessed by the intended audience using a variety of audio and video players *Vodcast*—videos created and shared via the Web using syndication feeds so that subscribers can be notified of new posts when available.	*Closed Captioning*—adding narrative and descriptive text to videos that display in a timely manner relative to what is happening on the screen
Training and Resources	www.apple.com/ilife/imovie/	www.google.com/support/youtube/bin/static.py?p=homepage&page=start.cs&hl=en_US

CHAPTER SEVENTEEN

SCREENCASTING

If you have ever taught in a physical classroom setting with a computer that projects on a screen in front of the class, you know how convenient that screen is for demonstrating to students how to navigate the Web; complete a specific task within an application (for example, merging from Microsoft Excel to Microsoft Word); and share other computer-based information. If we could only have that ability when students leave our classrooms or are logging on from a distance! Well, we do. Screencasting allows the instructor to record exactly what is on his or her computer screen and share it with students as a video file. Viewers see exactly what to do, click by click. This chapter presents the advantages of and considerations for using screencasts as a tool.

What Is the Tool?

Screencasting is a capability that is installed on your computer in the form of an application. The application allows a user to record what is on his or her computer screen, including the motion of the mouse and drop-down menus, along with audio narration if desired.

What Problem Does It Solve?

Screencasting helps with meeting instructional objectives and providing technical support to students. For example, a business applications instructor may use the tool to demonstrate to students the exact steps needed to use the table of contents feature in Microsoft Word correctly. Students can watch the screencast and then attempt the same task independently. Alternately, if a student contacts the instructor because he is unfamiliar with where to find specific information inside the virtual classroom, the instructor can use this tool to provide the student with technical support by recording a screencast of the steps for navigating to the needed information.

Is This Something Instructors or Students Use?

Although students could use the tool, the instructor and other staff members primarily use it to support the curriculum and provide technical support.

Is This Tool for the Novice, Intermediate, or Expert?

For the most part, the novice to intermediate user can easily implement this tool. If the purpose of screencasting is to add the captured video to another video production with edits, then more advanced skills are needed.

Is There Special Equipment or Software Needed?

Screencasting requires software that is responsible for capturing the screen in video format and a microphone for those wishing to narrate their screencasts as they record. Once the recording is captured, edited (if applicable), and saved in a universal video format (rendered), such as MP4, then the file must somehow be shared with learners over the Internet. Therefore, you must also have a way of distributing the final video as well. We provided one service for doing so in Chapter Sixteen—YouTube is a great tool for distributing your videos.

What Are Some Cautions About This Tool?

File sizes can get large and unwieldy depending on the length of the screencast. Short screencasts can easily be shared over e-mail or by uploading them to a video sharing service, such as YouTube. Also, some course management systems will let you upload your video directly so students can access it when they are logged into their virtual classroom. However, larger files require more Web space and possibly the ability to understand video streaming before sharing with an online audience. Remember, streaming occurs when you use a specific type of Web server that allows users to access your media files without having to download them to their local machines. Streaming technology also will let students start watching a video before it has completely loaded to avoid wasted time.

How Accessible Is This Tool to All Users?

The end product, a video file, can be made more accessible by accompanying it with a transcript or using an editor to add captions or narrative prompts on the video screen as it plays. Accessibility is determined by the screencasting tool you use. Some companies design products with accessibility in mind, whereas others, unfortunately, do not. Remember, though, that accessibility is the responsibility of the content creator. Therefore, it is important that you think of how you are going to make your videos in a manner that is accessible to many learning styles. For example, some screen-capturing software has built-in editors that allow you to add text prompts on the screen. You can use such tools to show where to click, for example, supplementing a narrated voice recording. Adding captions can be very expensive to have done. However, using titles and text prompts can help, as can offering the information in a fully text-based format separate from the video file itself. YouTube's closed-captioning option is fairly easy to use, but it takes a little time getting used to it.

What Additional Vocabulary Do I Need to Know?

Screencasting is synonymous with *screen capturing* and *screen recording*. These terms all refer to capturing the events on your computer screen in video format.

Can You Share a K–12 Example?

Let's say that you are teaching a sixth-grade, multisubject class, and you have created a Web site for students and parents. The Web site provides visitors with an introduction to who you are and provides important class information, such as themes, assignments, field trips, and more. To help visitors really get the most out of your site, you decide to screencast a virtual tour of the site and narrate it with audio cues on how to navigate, where to find the most important information, and how visitors can interact with you through the site. You post this screencast on the front page of your site so that parents can quickly learn how to use the Web-based resource in an efficient manner that will keep them up-to-date on what is going on in their children's classroom. Figure 17.1 shows you a screencast in progress using Jing, with the application's control panel in the bottom left for starting and stopping the recording process. The control panel does not appear in the final video.

FIGURE 17.1. SIXTH-GRADE CLASS WEB SITE TOUR (SCREENCAST) RECORDED USING JING

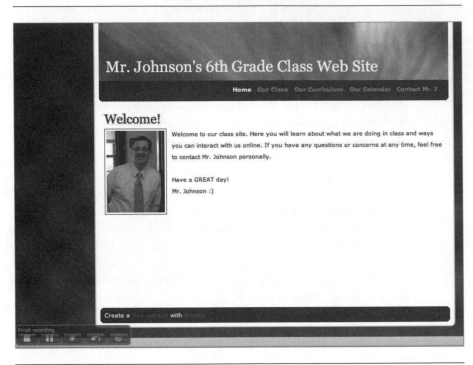

Used by permission.

Can You Share a Higher Education Example?

Imagine you are teaching an online education course when one of your students writes to you and says that he is unable to locate the digital drop box for an assignment he is ready to turn in—something not too hard for us to imagine, because this sort of thing happens a lot in the online environment. You can easily log in to the online class and then record the steps for navigating to the digital drop box and submitting the assignment. This screencast would only take about a minute's worth of video time, so it would be all right to send the video to the student in an e-mail. The student could watch the video and follow the same steps to submit his assignment. Figure 17.2 is an image of the ScreenFlow following the screen capture how to navigate within a Moodle course. The screencast editor is available when the screencast has been captured, and it allows you to edit your video by adding titles, zooms, pans, and more before sharing it with others.

FIGURE 17.2. POST SCREENCAST EDITING INTERFACE USING SCREENFLOW

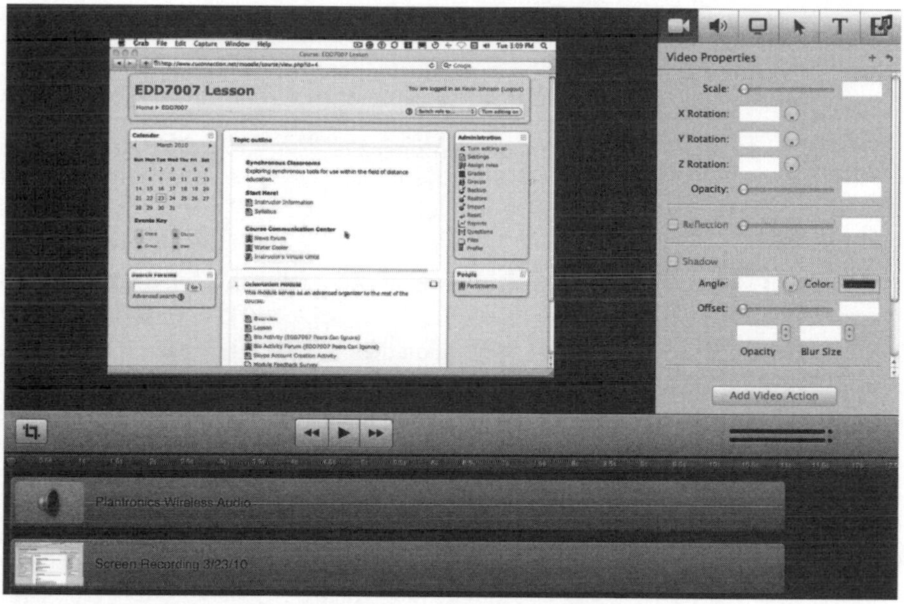

Used by permission. Telestream ScreenFlow screen capture software.

Where Can I Learn More?

To learn more about screencasting, we recommend the following resources:

ScreenCastsOnline! (2010). Mac Tutorials: ScreenCastsOnline. Retrieved from http://www.screencastsonline.com/

Udell, J. (2005). Secrets of screencasting. *InfoWorld.* Retrieved from www.infoworld.com/d/developer-world/secrets-screencasting-010

Currently Available Tools

- Jing at www.jingproject.com/
- Camtasia at www.techsmith.com/camtasia.asp
- Captivate at http://tryit.adobe.com/us/captivate/
- ScreenFlow at www.telestream.net/screen-flow/overview.htm

TABLE 17.1. DECISION-MAKING MATRIX—SCREENCASTING

	Jing	ScreenFlow
Type of Tool	Presentation of content	Presentation of content
Problem It Solves	This tool provides instructors with the ability to demonstrate course content and provide support to students needing help navigating the virtual environment.	This tool provides instructors with the ability to demonstrate course content and provide support to students needing help navigating the virtual environment.
Cost	Free	Inexpensive
URL	www.jingproject.com/	www.telestream.net/screenflow/overview.htm
Description	Jing is an application that allows users to take still snapshots or videos of their screens and then share those videos over the Web.	ScreenFlow is a screencast application that allows users to capture what's on their screen in video format and share it with others.
Platform	Mac or Windows	Mac
Best Used For	Creating and sharing content that is optimally delivered using video, such as an instructor's welcome message, video productions, and more	Creating and sharing content that is optimally delivered using video, such as an instructor's welcome message, video productions, and more
Level of Expertise	*Teacher:* Intermediate *Student:* Basic	*Teacher:* Intermediate *Student:* Basic
Cautions	In general, screencasts can generate large files that require substantial time to upload and download depending on bandwidth.	In general, screencasts can generate large files that require substantial time to upload and download depending on bandwidth. Also, ScreenFlow is a Mac-only product, which means that Windows users will not be able to use the product to capture screencasts.
Overcoming Cautions	Screencasts should be kept short and only focus on the necessary information. Jing provides each user with 2 GB of free storage space and 2 GB of free monthly bandwidth on their Screencast.com Web site, where you can easily upload your screencasts to share them with students.	Screencasts should be kept short and only focus on the necessary information. Further, although ScreenFlow is Mac-only, the final video can be rendered in a format easily viewed by persons with multiple operating systems.

TABLE 17.1. (*continued*)

	Jing	ScreenFlow
Accessibility Concerns	Jing is fairly user-friendly and uses your machine's built-in accessibility tools such as the built-in screen reader to help you navigate and use the tool. However, a transcript should accompany all screencasts, as with any video creation.	ScreenFlow is fairly user-friendly and uses your machine's built-in accessibility tools to help you navigate and use the tool. However, a transcript should accompany all screencasts, as with any video creation.
Special Equipment	Microphone for voice recording; speakers for playback	Microphone for voice recording; speakers for playback
Additional Vocabulary	*Screencasting* is synonymous with *screen capturing* and *screen recording*. These terms all refer to capturing the events on your computer screen in video format.	
Training and Resources	http://help.jingproject.com/	www.telestream.net/telestream-support/screen-flow/support.htm

CHAPTER EIGHTEEN

NARRATED SLIDE SHOWS

Are you someone who gets back from a trip, breaks out the slide projector, and invites everyone over for a vacation-sharing party at which you screen a million photos with themed music playing from your stereo in the background? Creating content-specific slide shows like this is now easier than ever. Of course, it is prudent to know your audience's attention span and create your slide shows accordingly. Just because you took five hundred pictures on your vacation, doesn't mean you have to share all of them. Your audience doesn't need to see the same image ten times from multiple angles or distances.

What Is the Tool?

Narrated slide shows or images are text-based slides (such as those created using PowerPoint) or still images supplemented with voice narration. The end result is a timed slide show that can run independently on a user's desktop or on the Web. There are some great new products out there, such as Animoto, which turns your images, movies, and audio files into a combined, sixty-second piece with fancy transitions and Hollywood-like edits.

What Problem Does It Solve?

Narrated slide shows allow the instructor to provide students with information visually and expand on what is on the screen with narration. This prevents the instructor from cluttering the screen with small text or relying on the students' ability to understand the full meaning behind a few bulleted phrases. Narrated slide shows also provide an alternative way for students to absorb content because they include audio. Viewers do not have to rely solely on reading.

Is This Something Instructors or Students Use?

This tool is easy enough for both instructors and students to use. Although we have seen it used more often for delivery of content from instructors to students, it is possible for students to use this tool to demonstrate their understanding of course content.

Is This Tool for the Novice, Intermediate, or Expert?

This is a tool that most novice computer users can pick up with little training or tutorial help. Of course, when asking students to use it, you should provide links to demonstration videos and other support materials.

Is There Special Equipment or Software Needed?

For narrated slides, both PowerPoint and Keynote (the Mac version of presentation software) have built-in options for recording narration and let you save your presentations as movie files. For images, you can use the same applications or another service, such as Yodio. A microphone is needed for recording voice, and we recommend purchasing a headset that incorporates a microphone for the convenience of not having to purchase separate devices.

What Are Some Cautions About This Tool?

We have seen narrated slides replace the traditional classroom lecture for distance students. Some of these presentations have lingered on for upwards of forty-five minutes to an hour. This tool is a great way to supplement content, but presentations should be limited to no more than fifteen to twenty minutes. Further, the best presentations require students to somehow connect the content back to the classroom. For example, if you are sharing images of the ancient pyramids with your students, require that they later engage in discussions about how the pyramids were made and what tools were used in the context of the time period in which they were created. These discussions could either be face-to-face or in an online discussion forum. It doesn't matter. What matters is that you engage students to think beyond the images and connect with the course content.

How Accessible Is This Tool to All Users?

Because this tool combines audio and video, you must remember that some students may have difficulties hearing or seeing the final product. Therefore, you may need to create alternative methods for delivering the same content, such as using full-text transcripts or closed-captioning, or use an alternative method altogether.

What Additional Vocabulary Do I Need to Know?

You don't need any additional vocabulary.

Can You Share a K–12 Example?

Think back to the opening example in this chapter about using photos to share stories from your recent vacation. Kids love to tell stories, and having them combine their stories with still images is a great way to engage them even more. As an elementary school teacher, you can ask students to tell stories of their families based on images that they share using storytelling applications, such as Microsoft's Photo Story 3 for Windows. Using this tool, students can upload images, insert titles, narrate, add background music, and customize motion effects between slides. Figure 18.1 illustrates a student's use of Photo Story 3.

Can You Share a Higher Education Example?

Imagine you are teaching Art Appreciation 101, and you wish to explain pieces of art based on their time periods by evaluating techniques specific to each artist. You could narrate still images of the art slide by slide in order to verbally explain each piece of art. You could then ask students to pick one of the pieces of art to critique in a discussion forum based on course content and personal taste. Figure 18.2 illustrates a Yodio presentation that mixes images with narration. Narration is recorded over the phone. Once the presentation is published, you have the option to either share a single link with your students or copy and paste the code necessary to embed the narrated slide show directly in your course management system or on your personal Web site.

FIGURE 18.1. STUDENT STORYTELLING ACTIVITY USING PHOTO STORY 3

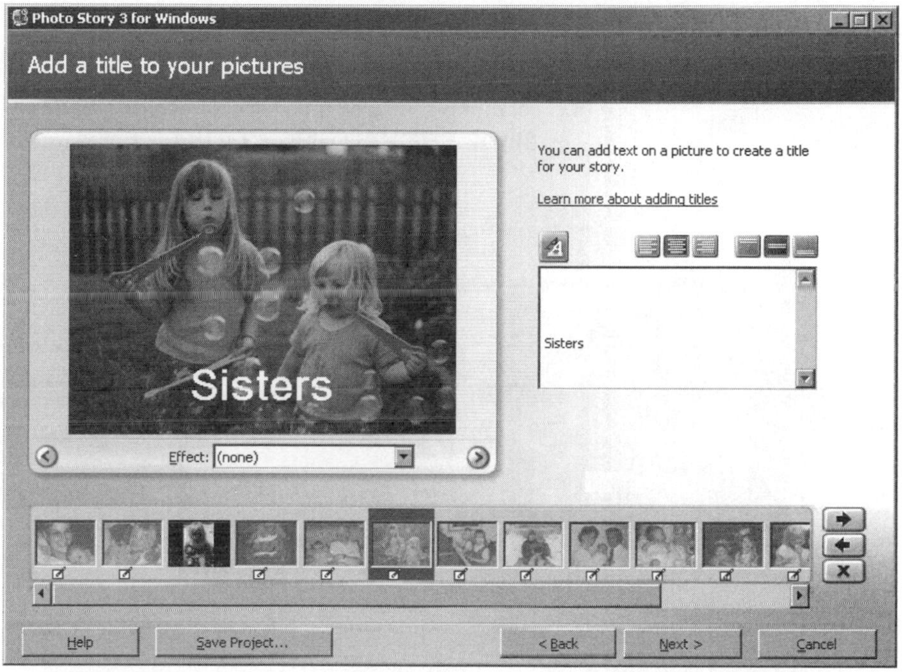

Used by permission.

Where Can I Learn More?

To learn more about narrated slide shows, please visit the Microsoft page on using narration with PowerPoint at http://office.microsoft.com/en-us/powerpoint/CH063500681033.aspx. Also, we recommend the following resource:

Bozarth, J. (2008). *Better than bullet points: Creating engaging e-learning with PowerPoint.* San Francisco: Pfeiffer.

Currently Available Tools

- PowerPoint at http://office.microsoft.com/en-us/powerpoint/default.aspx
- Keynote at www.apple.com/iwork/keynote/
- Yodio at www.yodio.com/

- Animoto at www.animoto.com
- SlideShare at www.slideshare.net
- Microsoft Photo Story 3 for Windows at www.microsoft.com/windowsxp/ using/digitalphotography/photostory/default.mspx

FIGURE 18.2. ART APPRECIATION NARRATED SLIDE SHOW USING YODIO

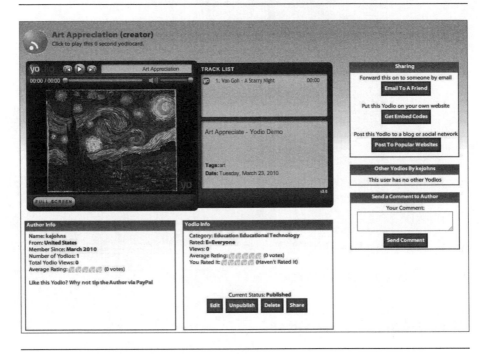

Used by permission.

TABLE 18.1. DECISION-MAKING MATRIX—NARRATED SLIDE SHOWS OR IMAGES

	Photo Story 3	Yodio
Type of Tool	Presentation of content	Presentation of content
Problem It Solves	This tool provides an alternative way to present visual content as a way of accommodating multiple learning styles.	This tool provides an alternative way to present visual content as a way of accommodating multiple learning styles.
Cost	Free	Free

(continued)

TABLE 18.1. (*continued*)

	Photo Story 3	Yodio
URL	www.microsoft.com/windowsxp/ using/digitalphotography/ photostory/default.mspx	www.yodio.com/
Description	Photo Story 3 is an application that allows you to create a slide show with your still images that include special effects, background music, and narration.	Yodio is an online application that allows you to add narration to uploaded photos and presentations and share these narrated presentations with students, colleagues, or friends.
Platform	Windows	Web, Mac, or Windows
Best Used For	Creating and sharing visual content in a more stimulating fashion than just still images.	Creating and sharing visual content in a more stimulating fashion than just still images.
Level of Expertise	*Teacher:* Basic *Student:* Basic	*Teacher:* Basic *Student:* Basic
Cautions	Be sure to keep presentations short and to the point.	Be sure to keep presentations short and to the point.
Overcoming Cautions	Create a storyboard and script and refine those until you have said what needs to be said in the fewest words possible.	Create a storyboard and script and refine those until you have said what needs to be said in the fewest words possible.
Accessibility Concerns	Microsoft Photo Story 3 is a Windows-only product, which means that Mac users will not be able to use the product to create videos. However, the final video can be rendered in a format easily viewed by persons with multiple operating systems. Otherwise, the program is downloaded to the user's computer and is accessible via the computer's added accessibility tools such as a screen reader (e.g., JAWS).	Yodio offers a variety of methods for recording narration, including using the telephone. Yodio also allows individuals to call in their audio using a 1-877 phone number to make creating the audio file easier than navigating the Web.
Special Equipment	Microphone for voice recording; speakers for playback	Microphone for voice recording; speakers for playback
Additional Vocabulary	None	None
Training and Resources	www.microsoft.com/windowsxp/ using/digitalphotography/ photostory/faq.mspx	www.yodio.com/public/ howitworks/faq.aspx

CHAPTER NINETEEN

SHARING IMAGES

As we began to write this chapter, Kevin's in-laws sent an e-mail from South Africa explaining their trip to a national park. They shared the experience of seeing exotic flowers, birds, and amazing animals, such as giraffes, rhinos, and monkeys, so close they could almost touch them. Although the description was nice, nothing made him more jealous than actually seeing pictures of these experiences, making Kevin's family feel as if they were there. Images help bring stories to life and can be a wonderful teaching tool. Plus, with today's technology, taking pictures and downloading them to your computer is as easy as ever. This chapter reviews Web sites that allow you to store and share images.

What Is the Tool?

Even though still images can seem less flashy than other tools for presenting content in today's world, they still have a place in education. Something as simple as a photo of the instructor can give distance students a feeling of human connection to complement the text communication shared between them. An image can also help any student connect with content in a more visual way, leaving less to the imagination. Don't get us wrong, we love imagination, but when an instructor is trying to express important details (for example, when describing the difference between similar architecture styles), sometimes the intimate details of the content are best described visually. For those of you with kids, you may also realize that your children can articulate past experiences better when they are provided with visual prompts through pictures. Kevin recently learned this when his son was better able to share memories of a trip to Disney World six months ago after reviewing pictures than of a trip to the local zoo only a week prior but without pictures.

A number of Web sites allow you to upload, organize, and share images. In some cases, the software also allows you to edit the images, and viewers can order reprints. Furthermore, some sites even allow visitors to comment on the images as a way of encouraging dialogue between the image owner and viewers.

What Problem Does It Solve?

Images help illustrate content. For example, think of an instructor teaching a lesson about how different aperture settings affect the quality of a photograph. He could easily use words to describe the importance of proper aperture settings and when to adjust a camera's aperture. However, showing students several photographs of the same image taken by the same camera with different aperture settings allows students to see the difference and provides them with visual cues for future reference.

Is This Something Instructors or Students Use?

Taking pictures in today's society is pretty simple. Most cell phones even come with built-in cameras. Most teenagers and a number of younger children have some kind of technical device that takes pictures, and with little direction they can upload these pictures to a variety of different photo-sharing Web sites. Therefore, this is something that both instructors and students can use.

Is This Tool for the Novice, Intermediate, or Expert?

For the most part, the novice-level user can easily implement this tool. There are even some digital cameras that automatically upload your images to a Web album at the push of a button.

Is There Special Equipment or Software Needed?

Aside from requiring a camera, you need to be able to transfer your images to a computer or a Web-based program. This might involve a cord or a wireless connection.

What Are Some Cautions About This Tool?

Some high-resolution cameras create very large files, which are not necessary for sharing images over the Web. Users must simply learn how to set their cameras to take pictures with a more Web-friendly resolution, which is usually explained in the devices' owner's manuals. Another thing to consider is the audience with whom you are sharing images. If privacy is needed, then consider a service through which images can be shared with a select audience using a password. This is especially important when sharing images containing pictures of children. You need to obtain parents' permission to post those images. Finally, although it is implied, it is probably a good idea for us to come right out and remind people that copyright and privacy for the subjects in the images are also concerns. It is important that any images you share online belong to you and do not infringe on the privacy of others. If you did not take the picture, it is your responsibility to ensure that you have the right to share the image with your class. In general, the photographer who took the picture owns the rights. It's also important that you stress copyright and privacy concerns with your students if you are going to have them share images as well.

How Accessible Is This Tool to All Users?

In general, the accessibility of a Web site depends on who created the site and whether or not the company is familiar with accessible design strategies. Otherwise, this tool is fairly accessible to individuals with basic knowledge of how to take pictures, navigate the Web, and upload files to the Web using standard Web interfaces. It is important to have such alternative materials as narrative descriptions or alternative assignments at the ready for students with visual impairments.

What Additional Vocabulary Do I Need to Know?

You don't need any additional vocabulary.

Can You Share a K–12 Example?

The preschool that Kevin's son, Garrett, attends engages the students in conversations about families and family backgrounds. Kevin's son is asked to bring in pictures of family members, and then to share stories about who is in each picture and how they relate to him. The children use printed images that are then pasted to construction paper to add colorful backgrounds to their collages of images. You can do something similar with older children, who can take digital pictures of their families and then upload them to a Web site with captions that explain each picture. As students grow even more sophisticated, you could ask them to take more abstract pictures that reflect who they are as people, and then have them supplement the images with narratives explaining the connections between them and the images. Figure 19.1 illustrates a web album in Google's Picasa in which the images and captions are specific to a class presentation about a student's dad. With a simple click of the mouse, the student can use the slide show link to have each image display on the screen one at a time as he talks about his dad, using the captions as presentation prompts. He might share this in a face-to-face environment, or over the Web by simply giving classmates the link to this specific photo album.

Can You Share a Higher Education Example?

A friend of ours teaches an online course on weather. Students are asked to take digital pictures of the sky and then post them with predictions of what the weather is going to be based on cloud formation and knowledge gained in the

FIGURE 19.1. STUDENT WEB ALBUM FOR PRESENTATION ABOUT DAD USING GOOGLE'S PICASA

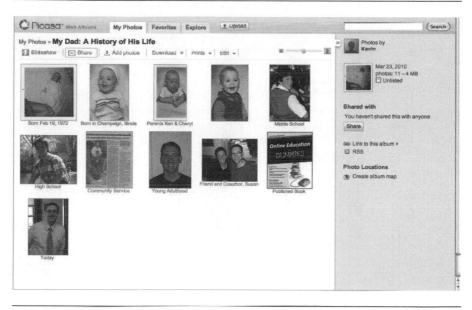

Used by permission.

course. Students then return to the course twenty-four hours later and report the actual weather and why their predictions were correct or incorrect. Figure 19.2 illustrates an image shared directly in the discussion forum by a student taking the weather course. The instructor or other students can now participate in discussion with this student by clicking on the reply link. The student can also reply to his own link as a way of sharing with the class whether or not his prediction was correct and why.

Where Can I Learn More?

To learn more about image-sharing tools, we recommend the following resource:

Goldfayn, A. L. (2006). *Going digital: Simple tools and techniques for sharing and enjoying your digital photos and home movies.* New York: Harper Paperbacks.

FIGURE 19.2. STUDENT POST WITH AN IMAGE IN A DISCUSSION FORUM USING MOODLE

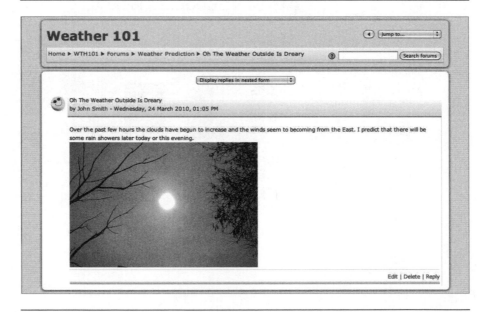

Currently Available Tools

- Flickr at www.flickr.com/
- Google's Picasa at http://picasaweb.googlc.com/
- Photobucket at http://photobucket.com/

TABLE 19.1. DECISION-MAKING MATRIX—SHARING IMAGES

	Google's Picasa	Moodle
Type of Tool	Presentation of content	Presentation of content
Problem It Solves	Sharing images keeps students from having to imagine what is being talked about within the course by providing the content to them visually. Visual information can also help reduce transactional distance when the visual content relates to the instructor or other students (e.g., images of self or surroundings such as home, children, pets, etc.).	Sharing images keeps students from having to imagine what is being talked about within the course by providing the content to them visually. Visual information can also help reduce transactional distance when the visual content relates to the instructor or other students (e.g., images of self or surroundings such as home, children, pets, etc.).
Cost	Free	Free
URL	http://picasaweb.google.com/	http://moodle.org
Description	This tool lets you upload your personal images to the Web and share them privately with invited guests only or publicly with anyone on the Web.	This tool lets you upload your personal images directly inside your online course in order to share with registered students.
Platform	Web	Web
Best Used For	Creating and sharing content that is optimally delivered using images	Conducting discussions surrounding shared images in the context of an online class or group in which participants are required to log in to access the discussion forums
Level of Expertise	*Teacher:* Basic *Student:* Basic	*Teacher:* Basic *Student:* Basic
Cautions	Everyone who is expected to upload images must have a username and password.	Moodle is an open-source product that requires the technical skills necessary to install and maintain it on a server.

(continued)

TABLE 19.1. (*continued*)

	Google's Picasa	Moodle
Overcoming Cautions	For K–12 environments, the instructor can develop a classroom album, log in for students, and help them upload images in a supervised environment.	There are some service providers, such as Moodlerooms (http://moodlerooms.com), that will host Moodle for your organization.
Accessibility Concerns	The Picasa Web site is fairly easy to use and has an average rating for accessibility.	Moodle designers have made accessibility a priority, and it is fairly easy to navigate and use this tool.
Special Equipment	Digital camera; wire to connect the camera to the computer	Digital camera; wire to connect the camera to the computer
Additional Vocabulary	None	None
Training and Resources	http://picasa.google.com/support/	http://moodle.org/support/ http://docs.moodle.org/en/Teacher_documentation

PART FIVE

TOOLS TO HELP YOU ASSESS LEARNING

How do we know when someone has learned something? As a teacher, do you test, give projects, ask for papers? How to you measure the outcomes? In this next section we shift our focus to tools that help measure outcomes for students through traditional testing or project- or performance-based work.

Remember that it is important for assessments to directly relate to the course goals and objectives. It's also important to remember when planning activities that the end result should be something measurable and observable. As a matter of fact, we will often develop an activity's assessment before developing the activity to make sure the activity itself connects well to course objectives. For example, if we want students to prove they know the acceptable components of a business plan, we might develop a rubric first. The rubric would articulate what makes up the measurable and observable pieces. Would they need to use specific vocabulary? Follow an organizational template? Answer certain key questions? Once this step is complete, we analyze what method provides the best means for students to demonstrate this knowledge (for example, essay, discussion, project, test, and so on), and then we create the assignment details based on the aforementioned information.

Other tools introduced in this section not only help the instructor assess work but also provide students with the ability to showcase their work online. E-portfolios provide students with Web-based resumes in which they can share their educational accomplishments; demonstrate growth to instructors; and provide visitors to their sites with overviews of their knowledge, skills, and abilities.

CHAPTER TWENTY

QUIZZES, TESTS, AND SURVEYS

There are several times when you as an instructor need to get quick information from your students. Whether checking their knowledge or surveying them to find out the best time to meet one-on-one, it's nice to have tools available that are quick, easy to use, and very inexpensive or free.

What Is the Tool?

Computer-based tests, quizzes, and surveys are great tools for instructors to assess students' basic knowledge. They are also great devices for students to review course content and test their own knowledge before having to demonstrate that knowledge for a grade. Even if you do not use tests, quizzes, and surveys within your courses, the same tools can be used when you need to collect quick information from your students. For example, if you are teaching an online class and wish to know when your students are available to attend a synchronous session with a guest lecture, you can send out a Web-based survey with specific dates and times asking them to indicate all the times they would be available to meet.

Web-based testing, quizzing, and surveying tools provide a variety of question types. Most include the basic short answer, true-false, fill-in-the-blank, multiple-choice, and essay question types, whereas others expand to matching problems, jumbled words, and other more complex question types. Other than with the essay questions, testing tools can check answers for correct responses and assign points accordingly. For essay questions, the instructor is required to log in to the system hosting the tool and manually grade each student's essay. It's also important to note that some course management systems such as Moodle and Desire2Learn come with these tools built in and will automatically transfer scores to an electronic grade book. However, when using other tools, such as a quiz made using Quia, the results are often shared in a downloadable file and then must be manually entered into the course grade book by the instructor.

What Problem Does It Solve?

For instructors who need information from their students fast, this tool can either test students for knowledge or provide a venue for collecting survey information. The tool also can help the instructor by automatically grading tests and quizzes and generating reports with student scores or survey results.

Is This Something Instructors or Students Use?

Although this is a tool that most instructors use to get information from students, students can also use it for their own data collection. For example, Web-based surveys are becoming increasingly popular as the tool of choice for doctoral students collecting data for their dissertations. For example, Kevin is using an online survey tool (SurveyMonkey) to collect data for his dissertation on what institutionally controlled components contribute to job satisfaction levels among distance adjunct faculty. By using a digital surveying tool, Kevin can collect more responses in a shorter time than he would by sending out physical forms and hoping to get them back—not to mention the money saved on postage.

Is This Tool for the Novice, Intermediate, or Expert?

Gone are the days of having to line up words with boxes and so on in an attempt to create your own paper-based tests, quizzes, or surveys. This tool makes it easy for any person with basic computer and Internet skills to create and deploy tests and surveys on a whim. For most products within this tool category, all you need is an account with the provider. An easy-to-use, Web-based interface then leads you through the creation process.

Is There Special Equipment or Software Needed?

Depending on how you wish to deliver your test, quiz, or survey, there are several products on the market that you can download to your computer that will allow you to print paper-based copies. To deliver online, all you need is a computer with Internet access and a Web browser. Most online tools require no downloading of software and are easy to use. However, as shared above, most vendors will require you to create accounts on their sites. If you are using tools that allow you to ask questions using audio or video files as a part of the question, students will be required to have speakers and the necessary plug-in to play the audio/video file, such Adobe Flash or Apple's Quicktime Movie Player.

What Are Some Cautions About This Tool?

Although online tests and quizzes are convenient, they are not always the most authentic way to assess students' work. Therefore, we caution you not to go overboard with this tool and use it as the only means of assessment in your teaching toolbox. As we have already stated, look at the course goals and objectives and challenge yourself to develop authentic assessments, such as content-based projects. For example, if you are a sociology instructor and you want your students to explain the methods used when studying groups and group formation, don't just ask them a multiple-choice question about the methods of study. Instead, ask them to actually participate in a method of study and report back to the class. Specifically, you could ask students to conduct an observation (one of the methods) and report back about the process, their roles as observers, and the results.

One of the biggest concerns with online tests and quizzes is how easy it is for students to cheat. Many instructors worry that the people taking their tests are not the students enrolled in their courses, or that students are using external resources in order to complete the tests. Depending on the resources available to you, there are several options for overcoming this concern. For example, some institutions require that each student either take tests on-site or take tests in front of a preapproved proctor that has contracted with the school. There are also tools, such as Respondus (www.respondus.com/), that will lock down the user's browser so that access to the Internet or other documents is prohibited when taking a test. Finally, there are commercial vendors, such as ProctorU (www.proctoru.com/), that monitor students from a distance using webcams while taking their exams.

How Accessible Is This Tool to All Users?

This will depend on the vendor's commitment to accessibility. However, many tests, quizzes, and surveys are delivered over the Web and are accessible overall. Be sure to have a backup plan ready if needed. For example, an oral exam, even if administered over the phone, can easily replace a Web-based test.

What Additional Vocabulary Do I Need to Know?

You don't need any additional vocabulary.

Can You Share a K–12 Example?

Kids love games, and many instructors use them as a teaching tool. Tests and quizzes do not have to have negative connotations, and with a simple change of the name, the same tools can be implemented in a fun and productive manner. For example, suppose you are a fifth-grade teacher teaching the states and capitals, and you want to reinforce what the class is learning with a number of activities. You can use the map to first focus on the states, and then begin introducing the capitals. One activity you may also implement in order to give students the opportunity for individual review is a computer-based quiz in which students can match states with capitals. By introducing five states at a time and asking students to match them with five possible capitals, you reinforce what students are learning at an individual level, and you can easily track each student's progress through the quizzing tool's reporting feature. Figure 20.1 provides an image of what this quiz, created using Quia, would look like in a Web browser. The instructor sends students to a link where they are asked their first and last names and then taken to the quiz. Quia records the scores, and the instructor can either get a summary of all students who have completed the quiz and their scores or receive details outlining each student's answer to each question.

FIGURE 20.1. QUIZ CREATED USING THE QUIA TEST TOOL

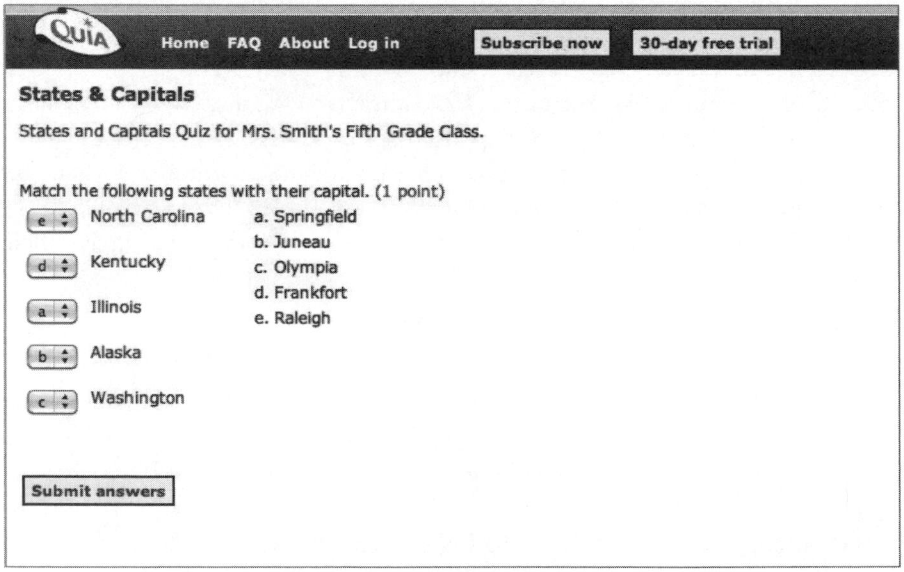

Can You Share a Higher Education Example?

One common use for testing and quizzing tools for adult learners online is at the beginning of the course to test whether or not students have read the syllabus and introduction materials. A quiz can also include a question that asks students to acknowledge that they have read and agree to the terms listed in the course syllabus and policy documents. For example, the quizzing tool would have a question like "What is the instructor's e-mail address?" as a way of making the students read the important information pertaining to the course. The last question might be a text question that asks students, "Please initial that you have read the syllabus, understand it, and agree to abide by the policies and procedures within it." Figure 20.2 illustrates an example of an orientation quiz provided inside the course management system. The instructor can choose to either give points for simply completing the quiz or award points based on correct and incorrect answers.

FIGURE 20.2. STUDENT ORIENTATION QUIZ CREATED USING MOODLE

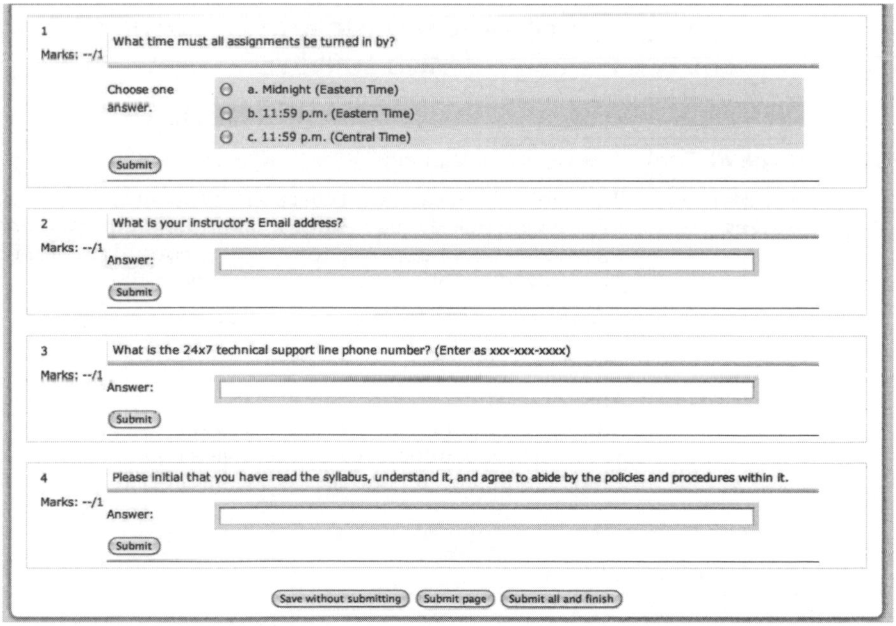

Where Can I Learn More?

To learn more about writing good test questions, we recommend the following resources.

- Conderman, G., & Koroghlanian, C. (2002). Writing test questions like a pro. *Intervention in School and Clinic*, *38*(2), pp. 83–87.
- Using Bloom's taxonomy to help write questions: Dalton, J., & Smith, D. (1986). *Extending children's special abilities: Strategies for primary classrooms.* Melbourne, Australia: Department of Education. www.teachers.ash.org.au/ researchskills/dalton.htm

Currently Available Tools

- Moodle at www.moodle.org/
- ProProfs Quiz School at www.proprofs.com/
- Quia at www.quia.com/
- SurveyMonkey at www.surveymonkey.com/
- Zoomerang at www.zoomerang.com/

TABLE 20.1. DECISION-MAKING MATRIX—QUIZZES, TESTS, AND SURVEYS

	Quia	Moodle
Type of Tool	Assessment of learning	Assessment of learning
Problem It Solves	This tool helps instructors collect information quickly such as knowledge about a specific topic or survey information.	This tool helps instructors collect information quickly such as knowledge about a specific topic or survey information.
Cost	Inexpensive	Free
URL	www.quia.com/	http://moodle.org
Description	This tool helps collect test, quiz, and survey information over the Web while also automatically grading and reporting results.	This tool helps collect test, quiz, and survey information within an online course while also automatically grading and reporting results to the tool's grade book.
Platform	Web	Web

TABLE 20.1. (*continued*)

	Quia	Moodle
Best Used For	Delivering Web-based tests, quizzes, and surveys for both assessment and self-assessment purposes	Delivering Web-based tests, quizzes, and surveys for both assessment and self-assessment purposes
Level of Expertise	*Teacher:* Basic *Student:* Basic	*Teacher:* Basic *Student:* Basic
Cautions	Overuse can bore students, and these instruments can replace more authentic assessment techniques.	Overuse can bore students, and these instruments can replace more authentic assessment techniques.
Overcoming Cautions	Use tests, quizzes, and surveys sparingly, and as only one method for assessing student work. Provide opportunities for students to practice on their own while supplementing the curriculum with additional assessment activities.	Use tests, quizzes, and surveys sparingly, and as only one method for assessing student work. Provide opportunities for students to practice on their own while supplementing the curriculum with additional assessment activities.
Accessibility Concerns	More complex question types, such as matching problems, might be difficult for students with learning disabilities or visual impairments. Therefore, you should make alternative testing (such as oral exams) available when necessary.	More complex question types, such as matching problems, might be difficult for students with learning disabilities or visual impairments. Therefore, you should make alternative testing options (such as oral exams) available when necessary.
Special Equipment	Java Plug-in; Adobe Flash; speakers for questions using sound	None if using the tool as is. If using questions with sound, students will require speakers. Additional plug-ins such as Adobe Flash or Quicktime Movie Player may be required if asking questions using animation or video.
Additional Vocabulary	None	None
Training and Resources	http://www.quia.com/ tutorials.html http://www.quia.com/ faq.html	http://moodle.org/support/ http://docs.moodle.org/en/ Teacher_documentation

CHAPTER TWENTY-ONE

RUBRICS AND MATRIXES

Tests, quizzes, and surveys need little introduction for students. Students know what to expect when taking a test using the computer, and very few directions or long explanations are needed. However, for such other assignments as projects, essays, discussions, and student-led presentations, students need a clear picture of what is expected of them and how the instructor will assess their work. Without this, students can feel lost and turn in work that doesn't directly relate to the course objectives, which should drive the purpose of each assignment.

What Is the Tool?

One way to help students understand how you will assess an assignment is by providing a grading rubric or matrix. A matrix is a detailed list of criteria for an assignment that can be broken down into categories, whereas a rubric gives a detailed description of each part of the assignment (matrix), and it also includes the points associated with each element—assuming the assignment is graded and points are distributed by weighted components. Some instructors choose to create rubrics and matrixes on their own using such applications as Microsoft Word; however, there are newer Web-based products that help instructors create these and share them with other instructors and over the Web. We review in this chapter the products that help teachers develop rubrics or matrixes. Examples include Rubistar and the Rubric Builder.

What Problem Does It Solve?

Oftentimes we, as instructors, give a brief narrative description of an assignment without fully explaining how it will be graded. Assessment rubrics and matrixes not only provide focus for students by providing them with a list of criteria by which you will assess their work, but they also help instructors ensure that assessments align with course goals and objectives. In some cases, as discussed in the previous chapter, the instructor creates the assessment first as a way of making sure the corresponding activity truly reflects the instructional objectives it is supposed to meet. For example, if the instructor is developing a project for which students are asked to create a database, he or she will want to be very specific as to what components must be included in the database. An assessment rubric would outline such items as the minimum number of tables, queries, and reports required within the database, and how many points will be awarded for each component. The rubric may also go further in helping the student focus on other non-content-related components as well, such as the number of points for turning the assignment in on time, penalties for late submission, grammar expectations, and so on. Some rubrics only provide the number of points possible, based on a project meeting all criteria, whereas others break assignments down into proficiency categories, such as excellent, meets expectations, and needs improvement. In this situation, each assignment component discussed above is then broken down according to these categories to give the students an idea of how the instructor will score the assignment quantitatively.

An instructor can benefit in many ways from using a rubric-creation product or service. Most services allow you to not only create your rubric but also store it for later use and share it with other instructors visiting the product's site. This can help save instructors' time by providing them with ideas of previously developed rubrics within their fields. For example, if you need a rubric for scoring a presentation and use one of these Web-based products, chances are good that some other teacher has shared a version he or she developed. Seeing others' work may inspire you. Depending on the product, you might even be able to use an already created rubric without having to build a new one yourself.

Is This Something Instructors or Students Use?

Instructors are responsible for using the products to create and develop rubrics and matrixes. The end result, the actual rubric or matrix, is used by the student for guidance on how to complete the assignment, and later by the instructor for guidance on grading the assignment. Again, we recommend providing this information up front as a way of being transparent in your teaching and helping students be more successful in the completion of the required assignments. It also helps when creating feedback. Oftentimes we will actually write our comments directly in rubrics documents and then send those on to the students as feedback.

Is This Tool for the Novice, Intermediate, or Expert?

Web-based products for creating rubrics and matrixes have been designed such that all an instructor has to do is log on to a Web site and complete a template using fill-in-the-blanks forms describing the categories and criteria for an assignment; the products then create the rubric or matrix automatically. Therefore, any instructor who has basic knowledge of Web navigation will be able to use this tool with ease.

Is There Special Equipment or Software Needed?

Depending on the specific product you choose to use, you may be required to create a log-in and password on a Web site or download software to the computer on which the tool will be created.

What Are Some Cautions About This Tool?

There are no real cautions with the actual tool itself. However, when writing rubrics or matrixes for assessment purposes, it is important to be as specific as possible. We have read several rubrics with vague language that don't really help the students understand what is truly expected of them in measurable and observable terms, making the tool more subjective in nature. For example, instead of using such language as "Students demonstrate exceptional critical thinking skills," use terms and phrases that define what you mean by critical thinking skills. Consider something like the following: "Students will demonstrate exceptional critical thinking skills by paraphrasing the author's main points, comparing these points to those of other outside authors, articulating whether or not they agree with the author and why, and explaining how the author's points apply to their own work-life environment." You can see that, in the latter example, students get a better picture of what is expected of them when completing the assignment.

One thing that some instructors worry about when creating assessment tools with such specific criteria for project completion is the idea of dampening creativity. We believe that providing students with a specific outline can seem a little "template-like," but that it in no way dictates how the student demonstrates understanding of the material. Each student will be able to complete the assignment using his or her own ideas.

How Accessible Is This Tool to All Users?

The accessibility of the product that creates the rubric or matrix will depend on the vendor's understanding of accessible design. The final product itself often is in a table format, which is less accessible for individuals with screen readers than is plain text.

What Additional Vocabulary Do I Need to Know?

You don't need any additional vocabulary.

Can You Share a K–12 Example?

Let's imagine you're teaching a book unit to your seventh-grade students. By the end of the unit, you want your students to work collaboratively in groups to create a book. You can ask your students to use a wiki in order to collaborate so that they could all contribute to the same document without having to send a file back and forth all the time. However, your students will need more information on exactly what you want for the final product. They will benefit from having a checklist of items to be completed in order to create their final product. You can make a rubric that outlines all the components of the book that the group must have as a part of their final product. Components may include a cover page, credits, a table of contents, an about the author page, chapters, a glossary, an index of vocabulary words used, and a back cover. Additional criteria within the rubric might include grammar, spelling, and meeting the submission deadlines. The rubric would outline each of these sections separately and describe what is expected in each. In this example, not only can students use the rubric as a checklist but parents can also use it to help their students at home. Figure 21.1 illustrates what it is like to create a rubric using the Web-based application

FIGURE 21.1. RUBRIC CREATED USING RUBISTAR

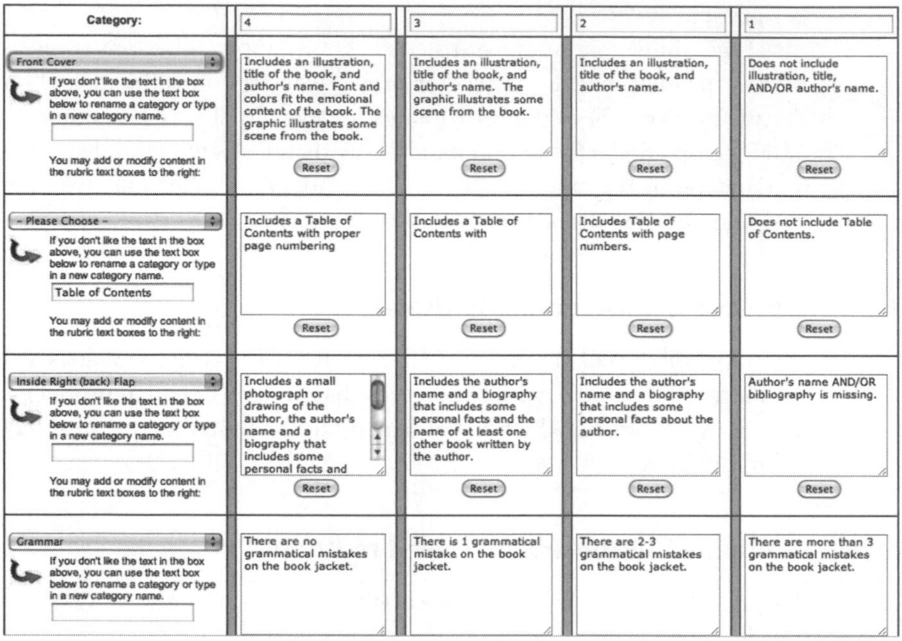

RubiStar, 2000-2010. Copyright ALTEC at the University of Kansas. Used by permission.

Rubistar, whereas Exhibit 21.1 demonstrates what the end result might look like when the rubric is printed for grading purposes.

Can You Share a Higher Education Example?

Many higher education classrooms require students to give presentations to the rest of the class, whether these are given face-to-face or using a Web-conferencing application from a distance. An instructor may want to set some very specific guidelines as to what is expected of each student during his or her presentation in regard to both content and performance. Therefore, the instructor could create a grading rubric that serves as both an outline for expectations and an observation sheet during each student's presentation. The instructor could share the rubric with students when first introducing the assignment as a way of helping them understand the grading process. The rubric will include such criteria as content clarity, effective communication, format, effective use of technology, and

EXHIBIT 21.1. EXAMPLE OF A PRINTED RUBRIC

Teacher Name: Mr. Johnson

Student Name: _____

Category	4 Points	3 Points	2 Points	0–1 Points
Front Cover	The front cover includes an illustration, the title of the book, and the author's name. Font and colors fit the emotional content of the book. The graphic illustrates some scene from the book.	The front cover includes an illustration, the title of the book, and author's name. The graphic illustrates some scene from the book.	The front cover includes an illustration, the title of the book, and author's name.	The front cover does not include an illustration, title, AND/OR author's name.
Table of Contents	The book includes a table of contents with proper page numbering.	The book includes a table of contents with page numbers.	The book includes a table of contents without page numbers.	The book does not include a table of contents.
Inside Right (Back) Flap	The book includes a small photograph or drawing of the author, the author's name, and a biography that includes some personal facts and the name of at least one other book written by the author.	The book includes the author's name and a biography that includes some personal facts and the name of at least one other book written by the author.	The book includes the author's name and a biography that includes some personal facts about the author.	The author's name AND/OR the bibliography are missing.
Grammar	There are no grammatical mistakes on the book jacket.	There is one grammatical mistake on the book jacket.	There are two to three grammatical mistakes on the book jacket.	There are more than three grammatical mistakes on the book jacket.
Spelling	There are three or fewer spelling errors on the book jacket. The author's name and the title are spelled correctly throughout!	There are three or fewer spelling errors on the book jacket, but the author's name is not always spelled correctly. The title is always spelled correctly.	There are three or fewer spelling errors on the book jacket, but the title and author's name are not always spelled correctly.	There are more than three spelling errors on the book jacket.
Comments and Total Score				

FIGURE 21.2. RUBRIC COMPLETED WITH THE RUBRIC BUILDER

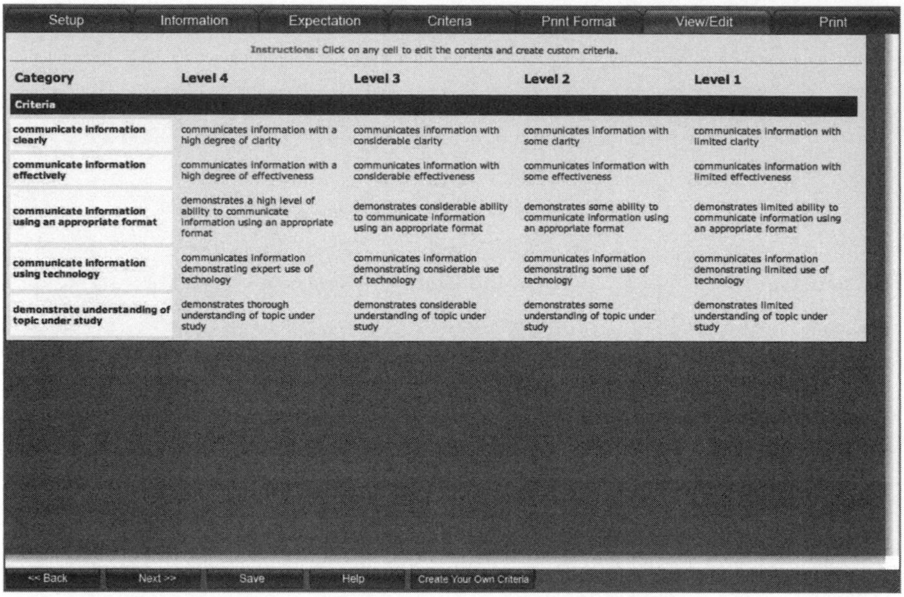

Used by permission.

content expertise. Figure 21.2 illustrates a rubric created using the Rubric Builder, which allows users to export created rubrics in either PDF or Word format.

Where Can I Learn More?

To learn more about writing good test questions, we recommend

Vandervelde, J. (2010). *Rubrics for assessment*. Retrieved from (www.uwstout.edu/soe/profdev/rubrics.shtml)

Butler, S. M., & McMunn, N. D. (2006). *A teacher's guide to classroom assessment: Understanding and using assessment to improve student learning.* San Francisco: Jossey-Bass.

Stevens, D. D., & Levi, A. J. (2004). *Introduction to rubrics: An assessment tool to save grading time, convey effective feedback and promote student learning.* Sterling, VA: Stylus.

Currently Available Tools

- Rubistar at http://rubistar.4teachers.org/
- The Rubric Builder at www.rubricbuilder.on.ca/

TABLE 21.1. DECISION-MAKING MATRIX—RUBRICS AND MATRIXES

	Rubistar	**The Rubric Builder**
Type of Tool	Assessment of learning	Assessment of Learning
Problem It Solves	This tool solves the problem of students not understanding what is expected of them and helps the instructor organize assessment criteria to make the grading process more efficient and less subjective.	This tool solves the problem of students not understanding what is expected of them and helps the instructor organize assessment criteria to make the grading process more efficient and less subjective.
Cost	Free	Inexpensive
URL	http://rubistar.4teachers.org/	www.rubricbuilder.on.ca/
Description	This is a free product for helping teachers create rubrics or locate existing rubrics based on category or title searches.	The Rubric Builder is an online tool that helps instructors build assessment rubrics and offers a variety of examples for word choice and structure.
Platform	Web	Web
Best Used For	Establishing and publishing criteria for assessing student assignments	Establishing and publishing criteria for assessing student assignments
Level of Expertise	*Teacher:* Basic *Student:* Basic	*Teacher:* Basic *Student:* Basic
Cautions	The language used within the rubric should be clear and in measurable and observable terms.	The language used within the rubric should be clear and in measurable and observable terms.
Overcoming Cautions	Revise vague terminology. For example, instead of stating "demonstration of critical thinking," describe what you mean by critical thinking in a manner that reduces subjectivity and allows students to truly understand what is expected of them.	Revise vague terminology. For example, instead of stating "demonstration of critical thinking," describe what you mean by critical thinking in a manner that reduces subjectivity and allows students to truly understand what is expected of them.

(continued)

TABLE 21.1. (*continued*)

	Rubistar	The Rubric Builder
Accessibility Concerns	Most of the rubrics generated use tables, which do not follow Web accessibility standards.	Most of the rubrics generated use tables, which do not follow Web accessibility standards.
Special Equipment	None	None
Additional Vocabulary	None	None
Training and Resources	http://rubistar.4teachers.org/ index.php?screen= Tutorial&module=Rubistar	http://www.rubricbuilder.on.ca/ learn.html

CHAPTER TWENTY-TWO

E-PORTFOLIOS

A ssessment should not be the sole responsibility of the instructor. Students should also participate in the assessment process through self-assessment and reflection. By doing this electronically, students can share their academic progress with instructors, department heads, graduation committees, and future employers. From an institutional perspective, accrediting agencies are asking programs to document student growth and learning over time by preserving student work in portfolios. The electronic versions of such portfolios allow students to select work across the curriculum, reflect on the process of meeting instructional objectives, and present their best work over time.

What Is the Tool?

Electronic portfolios, also known as e-portfolios, are Web-based repositories in which students can store their work, add descriptions and reflective comments, and share their overall academic progress with either the entire Web community or privately invited individuals. Whether the student is required to find his or her own e-portfolio product of choice or whether the institution pays for it often depends on how long the student has access to his or her school history.

For example, an institution that requires students to keep an electronic portfolio for graduation purposes may pay a vendor to provide services to students. Upon graduation, the students may be required to either purchase their own subscriptions to the service or move to other e-portfolio providers if they wish to continue sharing their work with perspective employers and other Web-goers.

What Problem Does It Solve?

Have you wondered what students completed in the class(es) before yours? Has their writing improved? What content knowledge do they have? How much have they grown in the specific content areas? Have they demonstrated enough mastery to earn the reward of graduation? E-portfolios help track students' academic progress at the course and program levels. From a program perspective, requiring students to complete e-portfolios throughout their academic journey requires a lot of preplanning and coordination on the part of the academic institution. It requires that an institution really think about and articulate the goals and measurable outcomes they want students to achieve. Planning at this level helps guarantee that the curriculum is developed collaboratively, which ensures that program objectives are met, assignments are not repeated, and the overall curriculum is developed in a clearly sequential and logical manner. This level of organization and development, when documented by student performance, also gives program graduation committees a clear picture of whether or not a given student has met graduation requirements.

E-portfolios also help instructors and graduation committees assess students' individual overall progress within their courses. By asking students to reflect on their own work via the e-portfolio system, instructors can get a clear sense of whether the students have grown and truly understand the concepts presented throughout the courses.

From a student's perspective, keeping a portfolio of academic and nonacademic work in an electronic format not only provides an opportunity to reflect on progress and learning process but also offers a point of reference when completing work projects that relate to assignments they have completed in their courses. The e-portfolio also becomes a tool for sharing skills and abilities with perspective employers, even particularly when applying for jobs at a distance.

Is This Something Instructors or Students Use?

An e-portfolio is a tool that both instructors and students use. In many situations, the institution purchases the e-portfolio service, and programs determine what artifacts from their courses are added to each student's portfolio. In this situation, assignments and their assessments are directly tied to the e-portfolio system, through which students sometimes even submit their assignments. Then instructors log in and provide comments on those assignments, which are immediately reflected in the students' e-portfolios and accessible online by pre-determined instructors and staff. Although a student's work is sometimes public for others to see, instructor comments and grades should be kept private so as not to violate the Family Educational Rights and Privacy Act (FERPA; http://www2.ed.gov/policy/gen/guid/fpco/ferpa/index.html).

Students use e-portfolios to showcase their work. We recommend that students consider creating e-portfolios even if their courses or programs do not require them. By doing so, they create public archives of their best work that they can share with current employers for promotional opportunities or with prospective employers when switching careers. A good e-portfolio is like a digital resume and includes an overview of the person creating it—his or her academic and professional goals, academic history, employment history, publications, internships, volunteer experience, and other pertinent information that demonstrates knowledge, skills, and abilities.

Is This Tool for the Novice, Intermediate, or Expert?

Most commercial e-portfolio systems use a simple, Web-based graphical user interface, but the setup process can be time-consuming and a little complex. From a student's perspective, submitting assignments, adding comments, and setting up permissions can also take time and require a little more technical experience. Therefore, this is a tool that requires intermediate skills at minimum to implement and use.

Is There Special Equipment or Software Needed?

If this tool is to be implemented at the institutional level, then a log-in and password with the correct access permissions are necessary. If you are asking students to create e-portfolios on their own, access to services that allow them to create their own accounts is needed.

What Are Some Cautions About This Tool?

E-portfolios are great tools for tracking academic progress. However, we have seen programs that require students to build their own e-portfolio using resources outside of the institution's control, and this practice can lead to a variety of challenges. For example, instructors may not be able to control the content that appears on each student's e-portfolio or to comment directly within the e-portfolio system due to privacy laws; also, instructors may find it difficult to provide technical support for applications with which they are not familiar.

How Accessible Is This Tool to All Users?

When evaluating e-portfolio systems at the institutional level, you will definitely want to consider accessibility. If students are choosing their own tools, many will not bear accessibility issues in mind, only concerning themselves with their own ability to access information. It is important that when introducing the concept of e-portfolios to students, you remind them that the more people who can access their information the better.

What Additional Vocabulary Do I Need to Know?

An *artifact*, in terms of e-portfolios, is an object—such as an essay, video, audio clip, or other academic assignment—that demonstrates a student's competencies in a specific area based on instructional or professional objectives.

Can You Share a K–12 Example?

Although physical portfolios are often used in the K–12 environment to help teachers get a sense of a student's previous work, e-portfolios are not as popular in the K–8 classrooms. They are, however, becoming more popular in 9–12 classrooms as a way of helping students prepare for their college lives. For example, a high school photography teacher may encourage his students to create e-portfolios in which they can share their work and the progress over their high school years. By doing this, students begin to build portfolios they can share when applying to liberal arts colleges, or when applying for scholarships specifically for arts-based students. Figure 22.1 provides a screenshot of a student's e-portfolio created using Pupil Pages, a tool specifically for K–12 users.

Can You Share a Higher Education Example?

Let's imagine that you are teaching an introduction course within the college of business. This is a great time to have students begin documenting the academic journey by asking them to create e-portfolios. You may ask your students to

FIGURE 22.1. K–12 STUDENT PORTFOLIO CREATED USING PUPIL PAGES

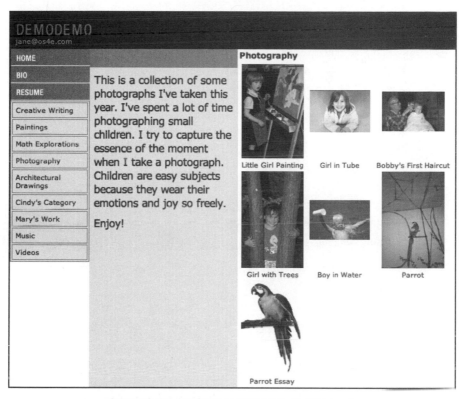

Used by permission.

develop the infrastructures of their e-portfolios by creating navigation menus; posting personal introductions, including their academic and professional goals; and inserting pictures of themselves. This sets the stage for them to submit academic artifacts and reflections throughout their academic careers. Let's now assume that you have asked your students to invest in and track mutual funds as their end-of-term project. This assignment could yield the students' first academic artifacts added to their e-portfolios, along with their own reflections as to why their funds grew or not. Figure 22.2 illustrates an e-portfolio created in the open-source system Mahara.

FIGURE 22.2. HIGHER EDUCATION STUDENT PORTFOLIO CREATED USING MAHARA

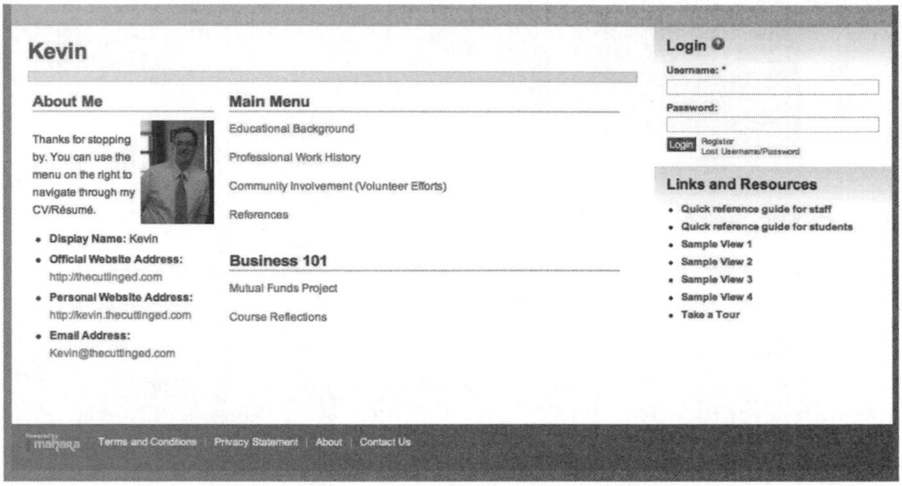

Used by permission.

Where Can I Learn More?

To learn more about e-portfolios, we recommend the following resources:

Buzzetto-More, N. A. (2010). *The e-portfolio paradigm: Informing, educating, assessing, and managing with e-portfolios.* Santa Rosa, CA: Informing Science Press.

Stefani, L., Mason, R., & Pegler, C. (2007). *The educational potential of e-portfolios: Supporting personal development and reflective learning (Connecting with e-learning).* New York: Routledge.

Currently Available Tools

- EPortfolio.org at www.eportfolio.org/
- Mahara at http://mahara.org/
- Pupil Pages at www.pupilpages.com/

TABLE 22.1. DECISION-MAKING MATRIX—E-PORTFOLIOS

	Pupil Pages	**Mahara**
Type of Tool	Assessment of learning	Assessment of learning
Problem It Solves	This tool solves the problem of how an institution can monitor overall student progress over a long period of time to determine growth and whether or not students have met the required objectives to graduate. It also provides students with a tool to share growth and accomplishments with other Web users.	This tool solves the problem of how an institution can monitor overall student progress over a long period of time to determine growth and whether or not students have met the required objectives to graduate. It also provides students with a tool to share growth and accomplishments with other Web users.
Cost	Inexpensive	Free
URL	www.pupilpages.com/	http://mahara.org/
Description	Pupil Pages is a Web-based e-portfolio tool created specifically for K–12 students.	Mahara is an open source e-portfolio system that provides users with the opportunity to share information and artifacts over the Web with an intended audience or the entire Web.
Platform	Web	Web
Best Used For	Focusing student assessments and allowing students to demonstrate their abilities to instructors, graduation committees, and employers.	Focusing student assessments and allowing students to demonstrate their abilities to instructors, graduation committees, and employers.
Level of Expertise	*Teacher:* Intermediate *Student:* Intermediate	*Teacher:* Intermediate *Student:* Intermediate
Cautions	It is necessary to establish the proper access and permissions setup. Instructor comments must be kept private to abide by privacy laws, such as FERPA.	It is necessary to establish the proper access and permissions setup. Instructor comments must be kept private to abide by privacy laws, such as FERPA.
Overcoming Cautions	Use a system that is provided by the institution so that there is more control over who has access to what; alternately, provide all comments privately outside of the e-portfolio system.	Use a system that is provided by the institution so that there is more control over who has access to what; alternately, provide all comments privately outside of the e-portfolio system.

(continued)

TABLE 22.1. (*continued*)

	Pupil Pages	Mahara
Accessibility Concerns	The institution will have more control over accessibility if the e-portfolio system is implemented across the institution. However, for this product specifically, accessibility concerns are minimal to those able to navigate the Web.	The institution will have more control over accessibility if the e-portfolio system is implemented across the institution. However, for this product specifically, accessibility concerns are minimal to those able to navigate the Web
Special Equipment	None	None
Additional Vocabulary	*Artifact*	*Artifact*
Training and Resources	www.pupilpages.com/site/support.htm	http://mahara.org/group/view.php?id=1

PART SIX

TOOLS TO HELP YOU
TRANSFORM YOUR IDENTITY

Okay, so up to this point, we have talked a lot about the serious pieces of teaching. We'd like to take a break from that and spend time sharing some of our more casual and fun tools. You can be anyone you want to be online, and it is said that the anonymity allows for enhanced communication. Individuals are not judged by gender, age, or ethnicity. With the tools we show in this section, you don't even need to be human! You can be a gorgeous fox, literally, in a virtual world. Or you could be a talking pineapple describing how sweet class is! The thing to remember is that even though you transform your identity, you're always the instructor. This part explores tools that allow you to transform your identity as you maintain a teaching presence. But to do this means we must, by default, provide our students the same opportunities to transform their identities. We discuss avatars, virtual worlds, and social networks as virtual venues for sharing content and interacting live.

CHAPTER TWENTY-THREE

AVATARS

Have you ever wished that you could bring your written text to "life" without needing the skills necessary to create video or animation? Or maybe you have the video skills, but you prefer to be behind the camera and not in front of it. Well, we have good news. There are free and inexpensive tools that allow you to transform your physical identity into an animated character that will speak your written words using either a computerized voice or your prerecorded voice.

What Is the Tool?

Avatars are animated characters that you can add to Web pages as a way of bringing a more personal, visual, and human element to a student's Web-surfing experience—even though some choose to express their virtual selves as dogs, cats, cartoon characters, and the like. Avatar applications allow you to create a character by choosing its human features, such as body shape, hair color, hairstyle, eye color, clothing, and glasses, as well as other accessories, such as hats, necklaces, and even tattoos. You can also choose to have the avatar look straight ahead at all times or follow the mouse movement on the screen with its eyes. Some avatar applications even allow you to choose specific body motions for your avatar, such as pointing, crossing arms, walking toward the screen, or twisting the body to give it more human-like characteristics. And these are just the types of avatars used for static Web pages. There are also moving characters that interact with others in dynamic, synchronous environments known as virtual worlds. These avatars are very human-like in looks and behavior. Their movement, speech, and personalities are those of the one at the keyboard controlling their virtual puppet strings. In this chapter we focus on the avatars for static, asynchronous use, and then we will dive into virtual worlds in the next chapter.

Once you have created your avatar, most applications allow you to type in your message for the avatar to say using a computerized voice, record the message using a microphone connected to your computer, or record your voice over the phone. The avatar then synchs its lip movements to the pattern of the text or audio file. Finally, the application provides you with the necessary code to copy and paste into your Web site so that the avatar appears on the page, speaking according to the provided script.

What Problem Does It Solve?

For some students, learning from a distance seems sterile and impersonal. The virtual classroom can be a very text-heavy environment that might make students sitting at their computers feel isolated and alone. One solution to this problem is the use of animated characters that provide visual and audio effects to content delivery. These animated characters are known as avatars. Although it may seem difficult to justify the use of avatars pedagogically, it isn't difficult to imagine that the use of such virtual characters has the ability to humanize the Web experience and increase student interest. This in turn can increase student satisfaction and success. As you will learn, we are not recommending that this tool be used to replace sixty-minute lectures, but rather that this tool be employed to enhance, with visuals and audio, what is often provided online using text only.

Is This Something Instructors or Students Use?

In later chapters we will discuss types of avatars and other virtual characters that students create. At this point, we are talking about a tool the instructor uses to create an animated character that presents information on a Web page as an alternative to providing the same information in a text-only fashion.

Is This Tool for the Novice, Intermediate, or Expert?

Novices can use avatars. They are fun and easy to use, and require few technical skills. Users will need to know how to copy and paste HTML code into the Web sites on which they want their avatars to appear.

Is There Special Equipment or Software Needed?

Most avatar applications are Web based and require the Flash plug-in, which most people have. Instructors who wish to record their voices also require microphones. We recommend using your own voice, because the computer voices provided by free and inexpensive tools are unflattering and do not add the personal touch your own voice can.

What Are Some Cautions About This Tool?

These are fun tools, but too much of anything can cause students to lose interest quickly. Therefore, instructors should be careful not to use avatars too much or use them to give lengthy lectures. Avatars are best suited for delivering short messages, such as welcome notes to students or introductions to new modules.

How Accessible Is This Tool to All Users?

Creating avatars can be difficult for individuals using assistive technologies, such as screen readers and breath- and mouth-controlled input devices. However, most vendors use Flash technology to deliver the end product, which can be viewed within most Web browsers. Again, though, always remember to accompany any audio or video component with a text-based transcript.

What Additional Vocabulary Do I Need to Know?

You don't need any additional vocabulary.

Can You Share a K–12 Example?

Let's assume you are a fifth grade teacher who has a Web site for your classroom with information for both students and parents such as information about the class, the curriculum, classroom calendar, and ways to contact you if needed. You could add a welcome message on the front page with an avatar that provides a more personalized message to those visiting your site. Because you are allowed to record your own voice as the message and design the avatar, you can make the animated character look and sound much like yourself. Figure 23.1 illustrates a SitePal avatar embedded on the instructor's Web site with a welcome message and transcript of the message below it. Visitors simply click on the play button to hear the instructor's voice come from the avatar while the avatar's mouth moves. This

FIGURE 23.1. TEACHER WEB SITE WITH A SITEPAL AVATAR EMBEDDED ON THE HOME PAGE

Used by permission.

avatar's head and eyes will also move—following the direction of the mouse when hovering on that page—giving the avatar an even more life-like appearance.

Can You Share a Higher Education Example?

To be honest, the higher education example in this case doesn't look too different from the K–12 example. It's easy to imagine welcoming new students to their virtual classroom and providing them with a brief audio narrative using your course management system or class Web site. You can log on to a service for

FIGURE 23.2. VOKI AVATAR INCLUDED INSIDE A COURSE DISCUSSION FORUM IN MOODLE

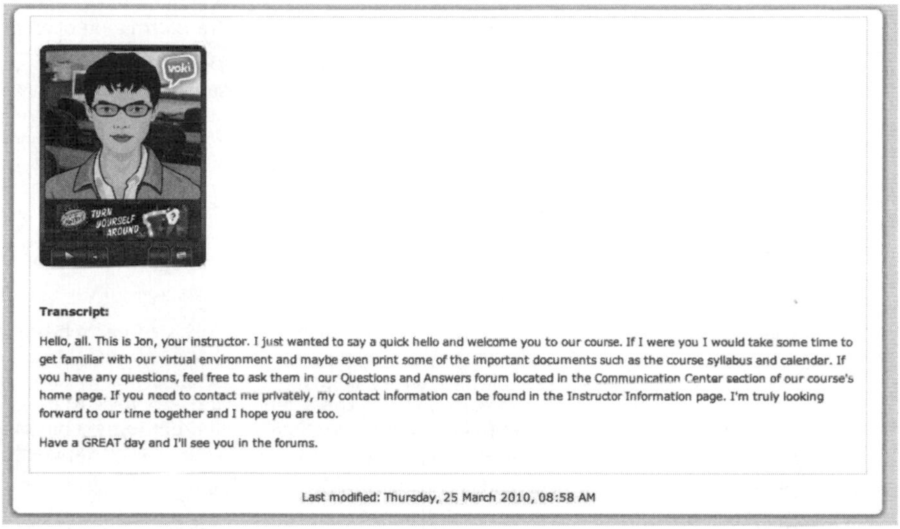

Transcript:

Hello, all. This is Jon, your instructor. I just wanted to say a quick hello and welcome you to our course. If I were you I would take some time to get familiar with our virtual environment and maybe even print some of the important documents such as the course syllabus and calendar. If you have any questions, feel free to ask them in our Questions and Answers forum located in the Communication Center section of our course's home page. If you need to contact me privately, my contact information can be found in the Instructor Information page. I'm truly looking forward to our time together and I hope you are too.

Have a GREAT day and I'll see you in the forums.

Last modified: Thursday, 25 March 2010, 08:58 AM

Used by permission.

creating your avatar, record the module introduction, and copy the necessary code to the Web site. Figure 23.2 illustrates the use of a Voki avatar embedded in a course management system. Notice the transcript below the avatar, included to make sure the content is more accessible to all learners.

Where Can I Learn More?

To learn more about avatars, we recommend the following resource:

Dyer, K. A. (2010). Voki—Avatars in education. *Squidoo*. Retrieved from www.squidoo.com/voki.

Currently Available Tools

- CodeBaby at www.codebaby.com/
- SitePal at http://sitepal.com/
- Voki at www.voki.com/

TABLE 23.1. DECISION-MAKING MATRIX—AVATARS

	SitePal	Voki
Type of Tool	Presentation of content Transformation of identity	Presentation of content Transformation of identity
Problem It Solves	This tool solves the problem of students feeling isolated and alone in a text-heavy environment by providing an alternative method for delivering content using animated characters known as avatars.	This tool solves the problem of students feeling isolated and alone in a text-heavy environment by providing an alternative method for delivering content using animated characters known as avatars.
Cost	Inexpensive	Free
URL	www.sitepal.com	www.voki.com/
Description	SitePal is a Web-based service that allows users to create personalized virtual characters and add voice to those characters in order to help personalize the Web viewing experience.	Voki is a free Web-based service that allows users to create personalized virtual characters and add voice to those characters in order to help personalize the Web viewing experience.
Platform	Web	Web
Best Used For	Delivering brief pieces of information online using a talking avatar	Delivering brief pieces of information online using a talking avatar
Level of Expertise	*Teacher:* Basic *Student:* Basic	*Teacher:* Basic *Student:* Basic
Cautions	Overuse can bore students and distract them from the learning process.	Overuse can bore students and distract them from the learning process.
Overcoming Cautions	Use avatars for delivering brief pieces of content, such as welcome messages and instructor introductions.	Use avatars for delivering brief pieces of content, such as welcome messages and instructor introductions.
Accessibility Concerns	Flash-based technology may make it difficult for users with screen readers to access menus, functions to turn on and off voice, and so on. It is important to accompany an avatar's speech with a transcript, and to set speech not to turn on automatically.	Flash-based technology may make it difficult for users with screen readers to access menus, functions to turn on and off voice, and so on. It is important to accompany an avatar's speech with a transcript, and to set speech not to turn on automatically.
Special Equipment	Adobe Flash Player; microphone for recording voice; speakers for playback	Adobe Flash Player; microphone for recording voice; speakers for to playback
Additional Vocabulary	None	None
Training and Resources	www.sitepal.com/support_ documentations	www.voki.com/create.php

CHAPTER TWENTY-FOUR

VIRTUAL WORLDS

In the previous chapter we talked about avatars that don't interact with the audience other than giving the illusion that they are talking to those visiting the sites on which they reside. It's now time to introduce you to a completely different level of avatar and virtual identity. Advanced applications now allow you to create a virtual presence in the form of an animated character and interact with other virtual avatars in environments that emulate the physical world.

What Is the Tool?

Virtual worlds are places on the Web that can either emulate our physical world or represent fantasy. Within virtual worlds, users get to create characters, come up with virtual names, dress them, and navigate in different virtual settings in a live (synchronous) environment. Avatars in this environment are able to interact with each other by engaging in conversation using text and voice while meeting in environments that resemble classrooms, libraries, bars, clubs, homes, and beaches.

In virtual worlds, individuals and organizations can purchase space to build virtual environments in which instructors, students, employees, family, and friends can gather for specific purposes. For example, several academic institutions have purchased space in virtual environments in which they have built virtual administrative offices, classrooms, libraries, and social organization meeting rooms. Paid staff are asked to create avatars and log in to the virtual world, where they interact with prospective students, instructors, and visitors from other institutions.

Then again, virtual worlds can be used without purchasing or building a space of your own. For example, if you want to take your class on a field trip to a hospital, chances are good that with some searching (maybe a lot of searching) you could find a virtual place to tour as a group. Another example is the common use of professional association space for short meetings; if you need to meet with a few colleagues about technology standards, our guess is that the space maintained by the International Society for Technology in Education in Second Life would welcome your group. Second Life is a popular virtual world where individuals and organizations can purchase real estate and build their own virtual presence including homes, offices, conference rooms, museums, and whatever else your can imagine.

Avatars in virtual worlds can interact not only with each other but also with a variety of content as well. For example, images, audio files, and videos can all be uploaded to the virtual world. Visitors to virtual worlds can also shop for clothes, electronics, and other items to take back to their virtual homes. In some cases these exchanges use fictitious funds, whereas others require actual money.

What Problem Does It Solve?

Many of our students are using the Web as a primary way of interacting with others. As an instructor, you may feel that your online course is not interactive enough to engage such social Web users. Virtual worlds provide an interactive, fun environment for students to meet with advisors, instructors, and peers in one-on-one, small-group, and large-group settings. As Dickey (2005) mentions, "This context builds on learners' real-world knowledge by providing a visual metaphor, or perhaps more aptly stated, a visual narrative of the course content. By using a 3D environment as a context for learning, the [Business Computing Skills 1000 Course] designers have created a place in which distributed learning is anchored in an environment that is both familiar and engaging."

Is This Something Instructors or Students Use?

Students outside of the academic arena often use virtual worlds as a way of connecting with others. Instructors use virtual worlds as alternative places for conducting classes, holding guest lectures, and meeting one-on-one with students.

Is This Tool for the Novice, Intermediate, or Expert?

Although these tools are not the most difficult in concept, it can take time to learn how to navigate and use all of their features. Instructors who want to use existing spaces for meeting can do so with intermediate-level skills. However, instructors wishing to build their own virtual environments will need to have expert-level skills to do so.

Is There Special Equipment or Software Needed?

Virtual worlds are Web based. However, unlike other applications that are completely served from the Web, virtual world applications often require you to download and install additional software on your local machine. For environments in which you can communicate using voice, you also need a microphone.

What Are Some Cautions About This Tool?

Using a virtual world requires technical skills that go beyond the basics and the time and patience necessary for learning how to navigate and interact within the environment. It is therefore important that instructors wishing to use such tools be prepared to train students.

How Accessible Is This Tool to All Users?

Some virtual worlds, such as Second Life, have worked hard to focus on accessibility issues, providing navigation through keystrokes and a variety of input devices. There is even a company in Japan currently working on technology that uses brain waves to control the computer in the hope of making virtual worlds more accessible to those who are paralyzed and unable to communicate orally or with physical expressions. However, when implementing such tools in the classroom, instructors will want to be familiar with the resources available to those who may need extra assistance, and weigh the benefit of convening in this environment against that of finding alternative methods for meeting the instructional objectives.

What Additional Vocabulary Do I Need to Know?

The term *sim*, short for *simulation*, is typically used to describe a geographic area in a virtual world. If you are on someone's island in Second Life, for example, you are on his or her sim. Sim can also be used to describe a virtual character.

Synchronous—real-time. In the case of virtual worlds, you log in to an application where you interact with others live in real-time.

In general there are no other vocabulary terms you need to know. However, each application may have terms and etiquette specific to that virtual world. It is thus important to check out help documentation and tutorials for each tool. For example, in Second Life, an *alt* refers to a person's alternative avatar—because a user can create more than one avatar.

Can You Share a K–12 Example?

One of the best K–12 examples shared with us was from a classroom for teaching children with autism. One of the instructional objectives of the course was to have students make a bank transaction in a virtual world by traveling to the bank on the subway, making casual conversation while waiting in line, making the transaction at the teller stand, and returning to the starting place. The classroom, based in New York, worked with LearningTimes (http://www.learningtimes.net), an organization focused on synchronous, virtual communication and collaboration, to create a virtual environment within Second Life that mimicked the streets, subways, and banks of New York. Students created accounts and practiced their social skills by navigating their avatars on a virtual subway to a bank, where they were required to stand in line and converse with other avatars, make virtual transactions, and return via the subway. This activity helped students with autism practice boosting their confidence in a safe, academic environment. Figure 24.1 shows several students waiting in line at the bank.

FIGURE 24.1. STUDENTS WAITING IN LINE AT A BANK IN SECOND LIFE

Used by permission.

Can You Share a Higher Education Example?

Let's imagine that you teach a class in which students are learning to be museum curators. Class objectives include developing exhibit themes and gallery showings for a given museum space as ways of demonstrating spatial organization and logic abilities. Obviously, most classrooms are not big enough for students to actually be able to do this, and instructors often have to settle for students demonstrating their skills via narrative descriptions of their ideas in essay form with a few drawings at most. However, in a virtual world, students could create their gallery in a visual format based on scale, using digital representations of the displayed work. You and the other class members could take virtual tours of each student's virtual project as if visiting the actual museum responsible for the exhibit. This activity would require that you and your students possess strong technical skills. First, there would have to be a virtual space in which students could build their exhibits. Second, students would have to know how to build the exhibits within the virtual environment. The time it takes to do this can be quite extensive, depending on the virtual environment you choose, and understanding these technicalities would better help you determine whether students could realistically complete the activity in the time provided. Figure 24.2 displays a museum with an exhibit installed outside the front entrance.

FIGURE 24.2. MUSEUM CREATED IN SECOND LIFE

Used by permission.

Where Can I Learn More?

To learn more about teaching in virtual worlds, we recommend the following resources:

Wankel, C., & Kingsley, J. (2009). *Higher education in virtual worlds: Teaching and learning in Second Life.* Bingley, UK: Emerald Group.

Virtual worlds review. (2006). Retrieved from www.virtualworldsreview.com/

Currently Available Tools

- Quest Atlantis at http://atlantis.crlt.indiana.edu/
- Fantage at www.fantage.com/
- Reaction Grid at www.reactiongrid.com/
- Second Life at http://secondlife.com/
- Teen Second Life at http://teen.secondlife.com/

TABLE 24.1. DECISION-MAKING MATRIX—VIRTUAL WORLDS

	Second Life
Type of Tool	Communication and collaboration Presentation of content Transformation of identity
Problem It Solves	Students are often using the Web for social interaction and entertainment, and online courses can sometimes take on a very text-heavy, isolating feel. Second Life is a virtual environment that provides a fun alternative for online synchronous meetings.
Cost	Free
URL	http://secondlife.com
Description	Second Life is a virtual world in which residents can create avatars and interact online.
Platform	Mac, Windows, and others
Best Used For	Creating an alternative environment in which classes and guest lectures can be held, and students can interact with the instructor and each other
Level of Expertise	*Teacher:* Intermediate *Student:* Intermediate
Cautions	The most difficult part of using virtual worlds is learning how to navigate and interact with other avatars and the environment.
Overcoming Cautions	A lot of time must be scheduled for training students in how to navigate and interact. Students will need access to tutorials and help documentation as well.
Accessibility Concerns	Second Life is more accessible to some than to others. Instructors will need to work with individual students to determine whether or not teaching students how to use the environment is worth the effort, or if an alternative instructional method would be more effective.
Special Equipment	Speakers and microphones for environments where interaction includes speech between characters
Additional Vocabulary	There are several specific terms used inside of Second Life as a part of its culture. The best way to learn this vocabulary is by accessing the link provided below. *Synchronous*—real-time. In the case of virtual worlds, you log in to an application where you interact with others live in real-time.
Training and Resources	http://wiki.secondlife.com/wiki/Main_Page

CHAPTER TWENTY-FIVE

SOCIAL NETWORKING AND YOUR STUDENTS' IDENTITIES

Social networks allow students and instructors to connect during and after formal instruction. Some of these networks are established primarily for professional purposes, whereas others are purely social. The use of social networks for instructional purposes is still a little controversial because of the social nature of the environment and the fact that users often create alternative identities within it. We know users who have posted pictures of people other than themselves, changed their name, or even their gender in order to participate in these environments more anonymously. However, this chapter explores the pedagogical value of blurring the boundaries between social and instructional.

What Is the Tool?

Social networking tools provide environments in which users can share contact information, photos, life updates, and more with either privately invited users or the entire Internet community. They also provide features that enhance interaction among users, such as discussion forums, polls, and calendaring and event RSVP tracking.

What Problem Does It Solve?

So many students are already using social networking tools to communicate with friends and family. The problem is that when they log in to their online courses, they don't often get the same feeling and can become easily bored. Also, some instructors don't have an institutional course management system already in place that they can use to host their online content. Social networking tools provide space in which instructors can quickly interact with students when more formal course management systems are not available. They also provide a place that is most likely already familiar to their students. With little learning curve, a teacher can use the products in this tool category to support either a full online class or a face-to-face classroom within a very short period of time. Instructors can conduct online discussions, make class announcements, invite parents into their virtual classrooms to see what their children are learning, invite guest lecturers to participate in question-and-answer sessions, and address privacy concerns by only allowing enrolled students to access the virtual space.

Is This Something Instructors or Students Use?

Most social networking tools allow users to create private space in which only invited users can view posts, participate in discussions, and receive updates from space administrators. Therefore, an instructor can use this tool to create a private space in which students can access class materials, participate in discussions, and interact with the teacher and fellow classmates in a more social environment. Parents can also be invited to this space to access information about what is going on in the class, missed homework, and other important announcements.

Is This Tool for the Novice, Intermediate, or Expert?

Social networking tools are easy to access and can be used by a novice.

Is There Special Equipment or Software Needed?

Most social networking products are hosted via the Web by the sponsoring company and only require a log-in and password. Therefore, the only equipment you need is a computer with Internet access and a Web browser. There are a few open-source products, such as Elgg, that an institution can install and host on a private server. This is more complicated, but it gives all ownership of the product and the content therein to the school.

What Are Some Cautions About This Tool?

There are boundaries that separate students from instructors, and many worry that social networking tools blur these boundaries. By giving students your social networking ID, you give them access to your personal posts, images, political affiliations, and other information that you may share under your personal social networking profile. Developing multiple profiles on the social networking Web site you use—one for personal use and the other for professional use—can easily address this concern.

Further, not every student wants to engage with social networking. Carefully consider whether student participation is required or optional based on course objectives. This also depends on whether or not you are using the product to supplement your course or as the main focus for your course.

Finally, from an instructor's perspective, the biggest piece missing from most of these environments is an online grade book. Instructors are required to be creative in how they update individuals on their performance.

How Accessible Is This Tool to All Users?

This is strictly a Web-based tool, and accessibility therefore depends on the vendor's commitment to accessible design. For example, Facebook has an accessibility team dedicated to ensuring that the tool is as accessible as possible.

What Additional Vocabulary Do I Need to Know?

You don't need any additional vocabulary.

Can You Share a K–12 Example?

It probably doesn't surprise you that the K–12 environment, due to security reasons, hasn't completely implemented social networking tools into the curriculum. However, in a quick inquiry among friends with teenage children, we found that teenagers are connected to an average of 1,200 friends, whereas our adult friends are connected to an average of 200 friends within their social networking environments. High school instructors can take advantage of this obvious use of social networking tools by teenagers by creating a private space in which course content can be shared in a more social manner. Developing companies, such as Edmodo, are creating student-safe environments for teachers to administer. These environments blend social networking with academic work. In Chapter Thirteen, we saw how Edmodo can be used for microblogging. A closer look at the same environment shows how Edmodo is really a social networking tool within which instructors can create a learning environment with enrolled users, blogging, calendars, grades, and other virtual learning resources. Figure 25.1 illustrates a K–12 social networking environment using Edmodo.

FIGURE 25.1. EDMODO SOCIAL NETWORKING ENVIRONMENT

Used by permission.

Can You Share a Higher Education Example?

For several pioneer instructors (those trying new technologies before their peers), who have no formal course management systems for storing course content or conducting online discussions, social networking tools offer a free alternative. For example, let's image that you are teaching Psychology 101 as a blended course. Your face-to-face class time is spent discussing theories, while you use a social networking tool to hold individual and group discussions; store important documents, such as the course syllabus; and note major assignment deadlines, using the tool's calendar. You can also use the announcement tool to send students important messages, which they can access from a variety of devices including the social networking tool itself, e-mail, and mobile phones. There is a welcome announcement on the wall and tabs that allow users to participate in discussions, upload photos, watch uploaded videos, and see upcoming events. This class can be set up as a private group, and students must be invited to join.

Where Can I Learn More?

To learn more about social networking tools, we recommend the following resource:

Kear, K. (2010). *Online and social networking communities: A best practice guide for educators.* New York: Routledge.

Currently Available Tools

- Elgg at elgg.org/
- Facebook at www.facebook.com/
- LinkedIn at www.linkedin.com/
- Ning at www.ning.com/

TABLE 25.1. DECISION-MAKING MATRIX—SOCIAL NETWORKING AND YOUR STUDENTS' IDENTITIES

	Edmodo	Facebook
Type of Tool	Communication and collaboration Presentation of content Transformation of identity	Communication and collaboration Presentation of content Transformation of identity
Problem It Solves	This tool solves the problem of providing a secure learning environment for instructors who do not have access to an institutional course management system and providing an environment with a more social feel familiar to most students.	This tool solves the problem of providing a secure learning environment for instructors who do not have access to an institutional course management system and providing an environment with a more social feel familiar to most students.
Cost	Free	Free
URL	www.edmodo.com/	www.facebook.com/
Description	Edmodo is a Web-based social learning network environment with education in mind. Features include enrollment privacy, calendar, grade book, assignment manager, blogs, and more.	Facebook is a social networking tool that helps people connect with others from a distance using profile pages, discussion forums, polls, announcements, photos, and more.

TABLE 25.1. (*continued*)

	Edmodo	Facebook
Platform	Web	Web
Best Used For	Creating alternative environments in which instructors can upload course documents and interact with students	Creating alternative environments in which instructors can upload course documents and interact with students
Level of Expertise	*Teacher:* Basic *Student:* Basic	*Teacher:* Basic *Student:* Basic
Cautions	Instructors need to set boundaries between their personal and professional lives.	Instructors need to set boundaries between their personal and professional lives.
Overcoming Cautions	Instructors can create separate profiles: one for business and one for personal use.	Instructors can create separate profiles: one for business and one for personal use.
Accessibility Concerns	Edmodo is Web based and accessible to learners with many learning needs and technical skills.	Facebook has an accessibility team committed to making sure their product is accessible to as many as possible.
Special Equipment	None	None
Additional Vocabulary	None	None
Training and Resources	www.edmodo.com/guide/	www.facebook.com/home.php?#!/help/?ref=drop

CHAPTER TWENTY-SIX

EMERGING TECHNOLOGY

Between the time when we proposed this book and when we finished the first manuscript, Google released its beta version of Google Wave, a product that blended e-mail, wikis, synchronous conferencing, maps, images, and more. The features and abilities changed daily as developers added new gadgets and applications. By the time we finished the edits, the wave had crested and Google released a statement that it would no longer develop for Google Wave. Simply put, Google had not seen the adoption rates it wanted with the product. Technology is a moving target. How can we keep up with what's coming next?

Staying abreast of current technological developments takes a deliberate effort, an open mind, and time enough to experiment. In this final chapter, we hope to leave you with outstanding questions you might want to apply as you inevitably run across emerging technologies. No matter what tool you use, it should always solve an instructional problem. Recall the central premise of our handbook: *technology tools must be used in the context of instructional design*. As technology tools change or emerge, your ability to evaluate them and their academic effectiveness should not waiver. We would begin with the following questions.

What Can I Do with This Tool That I Couldn't Previously Accomplish?

If you are truly following an instructional design process, then you are identifying instructional objectives based on a gap between what the learners currently know or can do and what you want them to be able to know or do. An emerging technology tool should be able to help you fill that gap in a way that you could not previously. If you cannot identify the problem or how the tool will help you address that problem, then perhaps you should not be using the tool. Just because you can does not mean that you should, and just because the tool is new does not mean it is better.

What Is the Learning Curve on This Tool for Me and My Students?

Learning how to use any tool takes time. Some tools seem to be easier to master because their features are familiar to us or they are not complex. For example, the text-editing features of a wiki look a lot like those of any standard word processing program you know (the capital "B" means "bold"!). Other technology tools may be more complex but come with exceptional tutorial support. We don't know many instructors who have the luxury of time to spend weeks or months experimenting with a tool. Therefore, consider the learning curve and how much time and energy you can invest. Then consider how long it may take your students to master the same tool. Do you want to use your instructional time to teach the tool or your instructional objectives?

How Accessible Is This Tool for Users with Disabilities?

Although we wish that the whole world would be sensitive to users with different abilities, not every tool comes fully accessible. This is an area that you should investigate carefully before putting any tool to use. Of course, you also need to take into consideration who your learners are, a standard front-end analysis in instructional design. Solutions to accessibility problems may be relatively simple, such as having an alternative to a video in the form of a text transcript.

Do You Have the Time for Mastering the Technology?

Our final word of advice is to set aside a dedicated amount of time each week to experiment with technology and see what it can do for you and your instructional objectives. As you do this, also look for a network of like-minded teachers. Few of us learn and master the tools alone, and the number of instructors who teach effectively with technology tools is growing! Tie into professional networks of technology-friendly teachers who can help you see the instructional applications of the tool. The same group may also help you troubleshoot any technical difficulties you might have. And finally, enjoy the process of learning and retooling. Working with technology allows us to experience the humbling position of being students!

REFERENCES

Agarwal, A. (2009, May 30). Web 3.0 concepts explained in plain English. *Digital inspiration.* www.labnol.org/internet/web-3-concepts-explained/8908/

Alexander, B. (2006). Web 2.0: A new wave of innovation for teaching and learning? *Educause Review, 41*(2), http://www.educause.edu/EDUCAUSE+Review/ EducauseReviewMagazineVolume41/Web20ANewWaveofInnovationforTe/ 158042

Allen, I. E., & Seaman, J. (2010). *Learning on demand: Online education in the United States, 2009,* www.sloan-c.org/publications/survey/pdf/learningondemand.pdf

Arms, K. A., & Camp, P. S. (1998). *The limitations of science biology—A journey into life.* Philadelphia: Saunders College.

Association for Educational Communications and Technology. (2001). *What is the knowledge base?* http://www.aect.org/standards/knowledgebase.html

Bell, A. (2009). *Exploring Web 2.0: Second generation interactive tools.* Georgetown, TX: Katy Crossing Press.

Betts, K. (2008). Online human touch (OHT) instruction and programming: A conceptual framework to increase student engagement and retention in online education, Part 1. *Journal of Online Learning and Teaching, 4*(3), http://jolt.merlot.org/vol4no3/betts_0908.htm

Brown, J. S., & Adler, R. P. (2008). Minds on fire: Open education, the long tail, and learning 2.0. *Educause Review Magazine, 43*(1), http://nct.educause.edu/ir/library/pdf/ ERM0811.pdf

Day, I., Wood, D., Scutter, S., & Astachnowicz, S. (2003). Interdisciplinary trials of synchronous, voice-based communication systems. In G. Crisp, D. Thiele, I. Scholten, S. Barker, & J. Baron (Eds.), *Interact, integrate, impact: Proceedings of the 20th Annual Conference of the Australasian Society for Computers in Learning in Tertiary Education.* Adelaide, December 7–10, 2003.

Dick, W., Carey, L., & Carey, J. O. (2001). *The systematic design of instruction* (5th ed.). New York: Addison, Wesley, Longman.

Dick, W., Carey, L., & Carey, J. O. (2008). *The systematic design of instruction*. Boston: Allyn & Bacon.

Dickey, M. D. (2005). Three-dimensional virtual worlds and distance learning: Two case studies of Active Worlds as a medium for distance education. *British Journal of Educational Technology, 36*(3), 439–451.

Downes, S. (2009a, April 13). Blogs in education. *Half an hour.* http://halfanhour.blogspot .com/2009/04/blogs-in-education.html

Downes, S. (2009b, December 13). Pew survey about the future of the Internet. *Half an hour*. http://halfanhour.blogspot.com/2009/12/pew-survey-about-future-of-internet.html

Duffy, P., & Bruns, A. (2006). The use of blogs, wikis and RSS in education: A conversation of possibilities. In *Proceedings of the Online Learning and Teaching Conference 2006* (pp. 31–38), Brisbane.

Educause. (2009, July 7). 7 things you should know about microblogging. www.educause.edu/Resources/7ThingsYouShouldKnowAboutMicro/174629

Elgan, M. (2006, September 14). The skinny on Web 2.0. *InformationWeek*. www.informationweek.com/news/showArticle.jhtml?articleID=161400004

Gagné, R. M., Wager, W. W., Golas, K. C., & Keller, J. M. (2005). *Principles of instructional design* (5th ed.). Beverly, MA: Wadsworth.

Hall, T., & Strangman, N. (2002). *Graphic organizers*. Wakefield, MA: National Center on Accessing the General Curriculum. www.cast.org/publications/ncac/ncac_go.html

Hall, V., Bailey, J., & Tillman, C. (1997). Can student-generated illustrations be worth ten thousand words? *Journal of Educational Psychology, 89,* 677–681.

Hanley, M. (2010). Discovering instructional design 11: The Kemp model. *E-learning curve blog.* http://michaelhanley.ie/elearningcurve/discovering-instructional-design-11-the -kemp-model/2009/06/10/

Hargadon, S. (2008, March 4). Web 2.0 is the future of education. *Steve Hargadon* (blog). www.stevehargadon.com/2008/03/web-20-is-future-of-education.html

International Network for Small and Medium Enterprises. (2010). *Glossary.* http://www.insme.org/page.asp?IDArea=1&page=glossary&IDAlphaLetter=T

Jonassen, D., Howland, J., Marra, R., & Crismond, D. (2008). *Meaningful learning with technology* (3rd ed.). Upper Saddle River, NJ: Pearson.

Jones, G. (2006, September 14). The World Wide Web: Past, present, and future. *InformationWeek.* www.informationweek.com/news/showArticle.jhtml;jsessionid= BG0Z0PW4JPCJBQE1GHOSKHWATMY32JVN?articleID=161400002&pgno= 1&queryText=&isPrev=

Kelly, K. (2009, August 6). Progression of the inevitable. *The technium.* Retrieved from www.kk.org/thetechnium/archives/2009/08/progression_of.php

Kelly, K. (2010). *What technology wants.* New York: Viking.

Lenhart, K., Purcell, K., Smith, A., & Zickuhr, K. (2010, February 3). Social media & mobile internet use among teens and young adults. *Pew Internet & American Life Project.* http://pewresearch.org/pubs/1484/social-media-mobile-internet-use-teens-millennials-fewer-blog

Mager, R. (1975). *Preparing instructional objectives* (2nd ed.). Belmont, CA: Pitman Learning.

Mager, R. F. (1988). *Making instruction work.* Belmont, CA: Lake.

McKenzie, J. (2003, January). Inspired investigations. *Educational Technology Journal, 12*(5). www.fno.org/jan03/inspiring.html

Moore, M. G. (1993). Theory of transactional distance. In D. Keegan (Ed.), *Theoretical principles of distance education* (pp. 22–38). New York: Routledge.

Morrison, G. R., Ross, S. M., & Kemp, J. E. (2007). *Designing effective instruction.* Hoboken, NJ: Wiley.

Nagel, D. (2009, October 28). Most college students to take classes online by 2014. *Campus Technology.* Retrieved from http://campustechnology.com/Articles/2009/10/28/Most -College-Students-To-Take-Classes-Online-by-2014.aspx

Palloff, R. M., & Pratt, K. (2003). *The virtual student: A profile and guide to working with online learners.* San Francisco: Jossey-Bass.

Reiser, R. (2001). A history of instructional design and technology. Part 1: A history of instructional design. *Educational Technology Research & Development, 49,* 53–64.

Saettler, P. (2004). The evolution of American educational technology. Greenwich, CT: Information Age Publishing.

Shirky, C. (2009, June 16). Clay Shirky: How cellphones, Twitter, Facebook can make history. *TED blog.* Retrieved from http://blog.ted.com/2009/06/clay_shirky_how.php

INDEX